SERVING FIRE

Passover 1998

Many
blessings
on
your
kitchen
and family!

With love,
The Snodys

SERVING FIRE

Food for Thought, Body, and Soul

ANNE SCOTT

Illustrations by Catherine Rose Crowther

CELESTIAL ARTS ◆ BERKELEY, CALIFORNIA

CELESTIAL ARTS PUBLISHING
P.O. Box 7123
Berkeley, California 94707

LIBRARY OF CONGRESS CATALOGING-IN-PUBLICATION DATA
Scott, Anne (Anne Leolani)
Serving fire : food for thought, body, and soul / Anne Scott.
p.   cm.
Includes bibliographical references.
ISBN 0-89087-739-4
1. Spiritual life. 2. Fire—Religious aspects.
3. Food—Religious aspects. I. Title.
BL453.S36   1994
291.4'3—dc20   94-26011
CIP

Cover and interior illustrations © 1994
by Catherine Rose Crowther.

Cover and text design by Sarah Levin.

"Chains of Fire" by Elsa Gidlow is reprinted
by courtesy of Booklegger Publishing,
San Francisco, California.

Printed in the United States
First Printing, 1994

2 3 4 5 6 / 99 98 97 96 95

To Stephen

and

to Eileen

CONTENTS

For no one owns or can own fire.

It lends itself.

Every hearth-keeper has known this.

Hearth-less, lighting one candle in the dark

We know it today.

Fire lends itself.

Serving our life.

Serving fire.

ELSA GIDLOW

PART I

SACRED FIRE

THE GIFT OF
THE BUDDHIST COOK

The minute I heard my first love story
I started looking for you, not knowing
how blind that was.

Lovers don't finally meet somewhere.
They're in each other all along.[1]

RUMI

 I AM WAITING FOR DINNER IN A GUESTHOUSE, along with fifteen other foreigners. The dining room in which we sit with its bare, whitewashed walls, clean wood floor, and glistening brass spittoon in one corner, could be anywhere in rural China. Throughout our travels, our hosts have planned meals catering to the Western palate to please us. Tonight's meal is very much like last night's: bowls of steaming white rice served with platters of various unidentifiable meats, lightened by an occasional strip of vegetable.

Early in the trip I asked for vegetarian food. At every meal I have been offered a bowl of rice and cabbage cooked in a Northern Chinese style. Sometimes a dish of peanuts has livened the cuisine. I expect no change in the fare, and wait patiently for my food. The others begin to eat. They finish their meal. I am still waiting. I wonder if my dinner has been forgotten.

I am ready to fill my bowl with plain rice when the waiter walks into the dining room carrying an array of dishes which he arranges before me. He returns with more until there are almost a dozen dishes on the table. This is no meal. It's an offering.

Everyone becomes silent before such artistry. Wild black mushrooms shimmer in a glossy red sweet-and-sour sauce, leafy greens are bright and fresh and warmed with ginger. Spicy bean curd is flecked with fiery red peppers. Tiny slivers of carrots, fresh-sliced bamboo shoots, and deep-fried gluten puffs float in golden sesame sauce.

I stare at the food in awe, my mind blank. The only sound comes from the ceiling fan rhythmically stirring the humid air. Then the cook enters and approaches our table. He bows low before me. He is grateful to me, he explains, because since his years as a cook in a Buddhist monastery, he had little opportunity to cook vegetarian food for anyone who appreciates it.

The wild mushrooms, he tells me, were picked in a nearby forest. The greens are from gardens known for the quality of their vegetables. He bows slowly, and thanks me once again. I stumble over my own words of gratitude as he quietly disappears into the kitchen. I never see him again.

I didn't sleep that night. The cook's reverence and humility sliced through years of protective hardness and caught me without warning. His food was saturated with love, and its nurturance was almost too much to bear. Bewildered and disturbed by the experience, I kept it to myself.

Six months before my trip to China, I had become ill while living in New York. I had always regarded kitchen work as a mundane activity to be avoided, but my deteriorating health forced me to examine my attitudes toward food and cooking. I became fascinated with Japanese and Chinese dietary philosophy, and learned to cook and eat in a new way. My health rapidly improved, and I gained a newfound respect for the healing potential of food and the power of the kitchen, the modern hearth.

I continued to study nutrition, in both Eastern and Western traditions, for the next two decades, learning food wisdom from teachers of many cultures. Later I began to share what I had learned about food and health with others.

I worked as a nutritional educator, counseling individual clients and giving lectures and workshops throughout California.

Despite years of exploring the outer world of nourishment, my inner hunger only grew more acute, and gradually my attention turned inward. Only then did I begin to understand what the Buddhist cook in China had given me: a part of myself that was beyond my conscious understanding. Something in me had been activated, awakened. It formed a question inside of me that led to a search for an answer.

It was this search that brought me to my initial understanding about nourishment. Real nourishment involves our whole being. The search for it takes us on a journey into ourselves, confronting us with our inner hunger. It leads us to the distinctions between our physical needs, our emotional needs, and the needs of the soul. Without this understanding, the desire for love, the fear of surrender, the rejection of parts of ourselves, all become entangled with the preparation and eating of food, and it becomes impossible to effectively nourish ourselves or others.

Learning to nourish, learning to be nourished, takes place at the hearth. When we tend the hearth, we open ourselves to receiving nourishment that feeds us—body and soul. This is possible because we still carry deep within us the ancient wisdom of the hearth, the knowledge of the sacred relationship between inner and outer worlds.

FIRE IN THE HEARTH

Love can both fiercely scorch,
and tenderly love and console.[1]

MECHTILD
OF MAGDEBURG

 WHEN WE LIVED CLOSER TO FIRE, when our lives depended upon the careful tending of the hearth, we had a symbol of the need for nourishment that lay deep in our souls.

How was it different when fire was central to our lives? It is probably fair to suppose that since humans have used fire, they have also carefully tended it, guarding the embers through day and night to ensure its survival. Throughout the Highlands and the Western Isles of Scotland, where peat was used for fuel, women performed a household ritual called *smooring*. The nightly ceremony ritualized the keeping of the fire to provide warmth for the following day.

The embers were evenly spread upon the hearth, which was generally in the middle of the room, and formed into a circle. The circle was then divided into three equal parts, with a small mound in the center. A block of peat was laid between each section, each block touching the common center. The first block was laid down in the name of the God of Life, the second in the name of the God of Peace, the third in the name of the God of Grace. The circle was then covered with ashes, sufficient to subdue but not extinguish the fire, in the name of the Three of Light.

The slight mound in the center was called Tulla nan Tri, meaning Hearth of the Three in Gaelic. When the smooring was complete, the woman in charge of the ritual closed her eyes and softly intoned a blessing:

THE SACRED THREE	N TRI NUMH
To save,	*A chumhnadh,*
To shield,	*A chomhnadh,*
To surround,	*A chomraig,*
The hearth,	*An tula,*
The house,	*An taighe,*
The household,	*An taghlaich,*
This eve,	*An oidhche,*
This night,	*An nochd,*
Oh! this eve,	*O! an oidhche,*
This night,	*An nochd,*
And every night,	*Agus gach oidhche,*
Every single night.	*Gach aon oidhche.*
Amen.	*Amen.* [2]

The woman's invocation arose from her love of the sacred, and her hearth was thus shielded, as was her household. Spirit and matter joined, and their union nourished the home.

That was the past. Now the hearth is hidden, and while our longing for meaning in our lives draws us to its fire, we don't know where to look or how to find it. The hearth is a symbol of the feminine that nourishes our soul and embraces our body. Rather than pushing us to transcend ourselves, the divine aspect of the feminine leads us into ourselves, and we are nourished by this journey.

It is beyond me to precisely define the feminine, for it is, along with the masculine, one of the fundamental mysteries of being human. Yet I know that it is felt in the body and in the heart, and connects us to each other and to all creation. It is a natural state, not unlike a state of prayer, that knows the sacredness of matter. Families, relationships, and the individual psyche are undernourished when the feminine is suppressed.

Though we may sense a deep longing for a life where the feminine and the masculine are balanced, there is no place to hold that longing, no container to keep it burning, no hearth. Many of us—men and women alike—cannot identify the source of this longing, and, unknowingly, misdirect it into the material world of consumerism, or the physical world of addictive sex, or the destructive cycle of drugs. Food itself can become a deadly substitute for the missing feminine in our soul, as evidenced by the frightening rise in eating disorders during the last two decades.

For thousands of years, the feminine in the form of a hearth or fire goddess was central to many cultures. Known by many names, her energy was remarkably consistent around the world. She was the keeper of the hearth and the knower of the spiritual nature of human beings. She was a doorway into the inner world of the soul. My own quest for an understanding of the hearth brought me to know four of these goddesses: Pele, the Hawaiian volcano goddess; Brighde, the hearth goddess of ancient Britain; Gabija, the Lithuanian fire goddess; and Hestia, the hearth goddess of ancient Greece. Each goddess can be viewed as a living current whose archetypal energy may be experienced inwardly.

Today, many cultures have forgotten her. The modern hearth is disconnected from the transformative power of the feminine and of the fire. Yet when we form a conscious relationship with the inner world of the feminine, we restore that which has been neglected and abused. When we love those parts of ourselves that have been denied a place in the sun, then the excluded element of the feminine becomes a creative and positive energy that assists us on our journey home.

Years ago, while deep in meditation, I saw a vivid image of a young girl's face. She was emaciated, mouth open in agony, crying out in a state of starvation. Although it was a terribly disturbing image, I was emotionally distant. I felt no relationship to her.

The next morning, while on a walk, I decided to recall her image and tried to communicate with her. "Who are you? What do you want?," I asked within. At first, there was no response. And then, in the wordless ways of the inner world, I began to hear her. She wanted me to listen without interruption or defense. Enraged that I had ignored her for most of my life, she had much to say. I agreed to listen. She continued with fury. Finally, she said in a quiet voice that what she really wanted was to be accepted by me, and loved.

I realized that this child was a part of me. I tried to embrace her, in my mind's eye, but she was so hideous, so repulsive, that I couldn't bear to touch her. At that point I opened to the pain that I had been unable to feel, and tears came quite unexpectedly. I was then able to touch her, just fingertips to fingertips. I hesitantly moved closer until I was able to hold her in my arms. The release of her grief was now mine, and to my surprise, her face became clear and beautiful. She said that she would help me in my life; she could show me how to nourish myself, how to find joy in day-to-day life. I needed only to remember her.

I had heard this voice before, but it was always a whisper, barely conscious, and one that I ignored in favor of a louder, rational voice. My intellect was intact, but I had lived for years without being present in my body. My civilized mind had rejected my instinctual nature. There was no place for the soul, and it was starving.

As we explore the meaning of the feminine in our lives, we learn that its nourishment involves nothing less than our own transformation. The exploration itself is nourishing, and simultaneously, also leads us to the source of our nourishment. We are shown how to live in the present, to be grounded in daily life, yet ever listening within.

Through honoring the feminine, we become keepers of the hearth; we tend its fire through our own ways of smooring. Instead of using blocks of peat for fuel, we place our receptivity, our gradual acceptance of ourselves, around the centerpoint of our being. The hearth fire renews us.

FIRE GODDESSES

Love is the essence of feminine consciousness—in men and women. It is the recognition and acceptance of the total individual, and loving the individual for who he or she is. The feminine is the loving container of all conflict, all physical and psychological processes. They must not be rejected, but safely, lovingly, contained.[1]

MARION WOODMAN

 I WAS BORN IN HAWAII but left the Islands when I was young. It was many years later that I became acquainted with Pele, the Hawaiian volcano goddess. During a week-long visit I felt strangely drawn to the lava fields. Every day I passed by the fields, wanting to walk in them, but I was afraid to go alone. Finally, despite my persistant uneasiness, the pull of the lava grew so strong I knew I had to overcome my fear.

I rose before dawn while the world was still empty and silent under a full moon. I found a path and walked in peace for a long while. Suddenly I panicked and wanted to go back. I turned around but saw many paths that all looked the same. I didn't know which one to take. I was lost. I could see nothing to guide me. It was clear that I would have to wait in the fields until sunrise.

To calm myself, I sat on a block of lava and began to meditate. A gentle sun finally touched my face, and I opened my eyes. I was stunned. All around me were hundreds of petroglyphs—beautiful, ancient symbols etched into the lava. I studied them in awe for at least an hour before the sun became too hot, and I turned back. A highway was now visible in the daylight, and it led me to my hotel.

That night I had a dream about one of the petroglyphs: a perfect circle with a dot in the center of it. The dot, I was told in the dream, was the center of love. Streams of love poured forth from this center into my body. A voice explained that the difficulties I was experiencing within my family would dissolve if I would be that dot in the center.

Intrigued by the petroglyphs, the next day I asked around and was directed to the hotel's security manager. I was told that he had been raised by his grandmother who knew of the old ways. Seated in his small office in the basement of the hotel, he told me that the circle with the dot had been used at the birth of a firstborn child. The infant's umbilical cord was placed in the hollowed-out dot in the middle of the circle and left there. It was thought to be a propitious sign if the cord decomposed without being eaten by birds or animals.

He also spoke to me about Pele as a personification of both aspects of the life force: the powerful creator of life, as well as the destroyer who makes way for new life. Volcanoes and lava beds are her territory. He referred to her as a passionate lover who reminds humans of their potential to love. Later that day, another Hawaiian friend explained the belief that it is unwise to cross Pele. She takes many forms and tests her people to see if they are loving. "That's why we are kind to strangers. You never know if it's Pele testing you," my friend said.

I then recalled my dream, and realized that I had experienced the archetypal energy of Pele. I understood that my dream was about my own journey. I could learn to love through a conscious relationship with the feminine. It would guide me to the dot in the circle, my own heart, like the hearth in the center of a house. Seeing Pele's dark side, I recognized that the path of love is not easy. The fire that nourishes is also the fire that burns our attachments and preferences. Anything that keeps us from truth will be thrown into the fire.

Following this dream, I began to learn about other goddesses of fire or the hearth. As I reflected about these goddesses, sometimes dreaming about them, I grew more conscious of the nature of the feminine.

Gabija

Venerated throughout Lithuania up to the end of the nineteenth century, the fire deity Gabija is still honored in villages to this day. The late Marija Gimbutas, professor of European archeology, explained to me that Gabija comes from the Lithuanian word *gaubti,* which means to cover or to protect.[2] She said that just as the fire protects the household, it is the duty of the mother or grandmother to protect the fire. The fire is carefully tended so that it will not go out during the night. Prayers are offered to Gabija, both in the mornings and in the evenings.

In earlier times, when fire was the only form of energy for heat or cooking, Gabija was considered truly vital to the welfare of a family. She represented the happiness of a household and was reverently carried by a mother into the house of a newly married daughter in the form of glowing coals for the new hearth, symbolizing the continuation of kinship with the mother's family. This was not a communal ceremony, but a one-house event, celebrated among members of the family.

In parts of Eastern Europe, the living fire is still protected by the mother of the house. Despite many cultural changes over the past few thousand years, the fire goddess has never disappeared completely.

Brighde

In the second century A.D., the great Celtic empire of Brigantia, which included parts of Spain, France, and the British Isles, took its name from

Brighde, which means Fiery Arrow or The Bright One. She was honored as the fire goddess,[3] but was also known as The Mothers or the Three Blessed Ladies of Britain.[4]

Brighde had three spheres of influence: the fire of the hearth and the smith, the flame of life within each creature, and the flame of divine inspiration. Brighde was the sacred flame at the center of the home and temple.[5] Priestesses kept a perpetual flame burning in the temple of Brighde. She was also revered in smithcraft, where the dissolving, creating, and shaping power of fire aided in the forging of metal tools. She presided over crops, flocks, and the world of nature. She is still called upon by women in childbirth and by those in need of healing. The honoring of Brighde is a living tradition that has continued, in somewhat altered form, into the twentieth century.

When the Christian era began, the influence of the goddess Brighde was still so great that her essence was carried forth by Saint Brigid of Bride, a woman who became bishop in sixth century Ireland.[6] Legend says that when Saint Brigid took the veil, a great flame leapt from the crown of her head to the very height of heaven. She preached equality of women and men, and worked with land reform to protect the rights of widows and poor farmers. When she needed renewal, she spent time alone in nature. Saint Brigid established a monastery for both women and men in Kildare, and like the priestesses before them, the Christian nuns continued the tending of the perpetual flame. This flame was extinguished in 1220, when the Archbishop of Dublin decided that the fire-cult was pagan. After his death, the nuns relit the flame. It continued burning until the Reformation in the sixteenth century.[7]

Hestia

In ancient Greece, the presence of the goddess Hestia was felt not only in the hearth fire that provided heat for the preparation of food, but also in the spiritual lives of her followers. She was described as a living presence in the flame at the center of home, temple and city. Like Gabija in Lithuania, Hestia made both home and temple sacred. The hearth fire symbolized a continuum and was always carefully transferred to a newly married couple's house. The bride's mother carried a torch from her own fire and, by lighting the first fire in her daughter's house, transformed it into a home.

Hestia's influence went far beyond the household. Each city-state in Greece had a common hearth with a sacred fire in the main hall. Colonists took the sacred fire from their home city with them and used it to light the fire of a new settlement.

During the Roman empire, Hestia was known as Vesta. Her power, too, extended over altars and hearths. All prayers and offerings began and ended with her "because she is the guardian of the innermost things," according to Cicero.[8]

Philosophers known as the Pythagoreans taught about Hestia in ancient Greece. While most of their teaching was oral, one Pythagorean, Philolaus, who lived in the second half of the fifth century B.C., wrote about Hestia.[9] For the Pythagoreans, everything was divine, and they explained everything—cosmology, astronomy, geometry, biology—in terms of divinities. Philolaus described Hestia as "the first thing to be fitted together, the One in the middle of the sphere."[10]

Dr. Peter Kingsley, lecturer of ancient Greek literature and philosophy at London University, explains, "For the Pythagoreans, Hestia was, (1), in the universe or 'macrocosm', the "central fire": the fiery body at the center of the universe around which all other cosmic bodies (including the sun and our earth) revolve. It was the generative, creative principle of the universe. And, (2), in the 'microcosm' or human body, Hestia corresponded to the fiery, generative principle that creates and maintains the body. She was located in the navel *(omphalos).*"[11]

Unlike other gods and goddesses in Greek mythology, Hestia was less known through statues. Her significance was found exclusively in rituals and her symbol was the circle, the round hearth. Hestia had no consort, and yet she was often paired with the pillar of Hermes, whose likeness was always located at the threshold and who shared a powerful influence on daily life. Hestia was occasionally portrayed in sculpture and on vases, often, but not always, in the company of Hermes.

The early representation of Hermes in the Greco-Roman world was in the form of a "herm"—a four-cornered pillar often with a bust of Hermes on top. In ancient Athens these pillars proliferated as boundary marks, signposts, and particularly as shrines of protection at crossroads. Hermes was "the one at the entrance" who mediated between the worlds of night and day, the worlds of divinity and humanity.[12]

While Hestia's fire offered sanctuary, a place to come home to, Hermes drew people to the fire and helped to contain it, keeping boundaries safe. He brought change by guiding souls to the fire of transformation and nourishment—then leaving them to Hestia's influence.

Jungian analyst Jean Shinoda Bolen writes of the synergistic relationship of Hestia and Hermes: "From Greek times on, Western cultures have emphasized duality, a splitting or differentiation between masculine and feminine, mind and body, logos and eros, active and receptive, which then all became superior and inferior values, respectively. When Hestia and Hermes were both honored in households and temples, Hestian feminine values were, if anything, the more important—she received the highest honors. At that time, there was a complementary duality. Hestia has since then been devalued and forgotten. Her sacred fires are no longer tended, and what she represented is no longer honored."[13]

These archetypes hold tremendous power, and yet our understanding of them remains an intellectual exercise unless we experience their meaning in our daily lives. How do we bridge the distance that separates intellect from inner experience? First, we must consider our individual feelings in relationship to these goddesses. These feelings lead us to meaning, and gradually the power of these archetypes becomes our own.

TENDING THE HEARTH

The hearth was in the midst of the dwelling; that hearth was to each member of the household, as it were, an umbilicum orbis, or navel of the earth...hearth being only another form of earth, as in the German erde and herde.[1]

W. R. LETHABY

 OUTSIDE A SUPERMARKET, I overhear several high school girls talking about their family mealtime patterns. They agree that they rarely eat meals with their families. Every family member has a different schedule. "I'd like to eat with my family more often," one says wistfully. The others nod. "Do you know how to cook?" another asks. "I know how to put a burrito in the microwave and that's about it. I'd like to know how to cook. But I guess this is fine."

There is a sadness in their voices, then they become silent. They avoid each other's eyes, shrug their shoulders and change the subject. I sense their fear. They are afraid they're missing something very important, and are powerless to do anything about it. These teenagers already feel the inner impoverishment that occurs when our outer lives are unconnected to our souls.

It is a lack of focus rather than a lack of time that keeps us from tending the hearth today. In Latin, *focus* means hearth. In our era of rapid change we have lost focus, lost the center, and can only regain it through inner attention.

Honoring the hearth is a state of being that radiates outward, nourishing other parts of our lives. The hearth keeper holds both the inner and outer worlds simultaneously. Daily actions, thoughts, and feelings provide kindling for the fire of the hearth. We must start with what is conscious, and slowly allow for greater awareness. We must focus our attention inward while we live in the world with families, jobs, and daily responsibilities.

The significance of Hermes and Hestia indicates what it means to connect the inner and outer worlds. Consider Hermes as the actor in the world. He goes to work, drives carpool, attends meetings, dines out, goes to the movies, and pays bills. We may be less familiar with Hermes as guide and protector. Standing at the threshold, he protects the sanctuary and honors its boundaries. Hestia beckons us inside, guiding us toward the peace that comes from re-membering the hearth. Back and forth we go, through the door where Hermes stands guard, until we find that, one day, we move more easily to and fro. The door hinges are oiled with our devotion, our focus on the hearth. We can live amid the activity in the world and yet be nourished and sustained by the sacred flame inside.

Like Hermes, we bring ourselves, with great respect, to our own inner temple fires for nourishment. We stand guard within our own inner world by becoming the observer. We learn to fulfill our function as the watcher by be-coming aware of thoughts that usually go through our minds unnoticed. We see ourselves as we are, without dressing up or hiding our blemishes. The one who watches is the priest or priestess of the hearth. The watcher is the con-scious aspect of our being that allows the safe exploration of our inner world. The watcher protects us; in fact, we can't nourish ourselves fully without de-veloping this self-observer.

For me, learning to use the self-observer has been a lesson in composting. I have always been fascinated by the compost pile just outside our garden. It contains bits of old food, thick and gnarled weed roots, rotting flowers, egg shells. It seethes with life. Over time, with moisture and heat, this decaying pile of unwanted organic matter becomes sweet-smelling, fertile, crumbly compost. And so it is with the discarded parts of ourselves that we have swept under the carpet. Under the watchful eye of the self-observer, all that we have rejected, denied, and hidden, is exactly what can nurture our growth.

Some years back, I returned to the piano after a twenty-two year break. Even after a year of lessons, my progress was distressingly slow. I could hear beautiful and complex music in my head, but what came out from my fingers seemed ungainly and simple. I abhorred the bumbling musician in me who was always concerned with the goal rather than the process. I couldn't bear to see my imperfections.

My teacher continually pushed me to the edge of my skill, stretching me beyond my safety zone. "Don't recoil when you make a mistake," he said to me one day. "Just say, 'Oh, I've made a mistake. Now I know where there is a gap in my knowledge.'" All this time I had been judging myself without mercy.

The intention, in developing the self-observer and watching the mind, is to go beyond the illusions of who we think we are, pushing ourselves to the edge of self-knowledge. We can learn to see ourselves through what is called "the eye of the heart" or, like the Hawaiian petroglyph, from the dot in the center. The watcher accepts us as we are, without judgement. It loves us despite our clumsiness, our fears, our lack of skill. What has been rejected, either by others or by ourselves, can surface and be transformed in this loving acceptance. One day during a piano lesson, I explained to my teacher that I must be musically impaired, and questioned the value of further lessons. He didn't answer. Instead, he wrote the words "Secret Jewel" on my music notebook. He then flipped back the pages to an earlier lesson and carefully made an asterisk with the following words: "Kindness to Self." I continued to study the piano, but it took a long time to learn this lesson.

For nine years, we have been double-digging our vegetable garden. By now, one would think that all the stones and weeds would be gone. This year, however, we found two rust-colored stone arrowheads in the soil, left from a time when the Pomo Indians walked this land. Hearth work is similar; we sift through our thoughts, slowly, watching carefully, and when the time is right, unconscious thoughts rise up and are "found" by the watcher. The thoughts have always been there; they were just unnoticed.

As we grow accustomed to this process of inner watching, we gradually awaken to ways in which we block our own nourishment. These blocks may arise from our early conditioning or from a childhood wounding. Even though we may be trying to eat well, this conditioning can unwittingly sabotage our efforts. We can be blocked by feelings like "I don't deserve love," "I don't like my body," or "I'm superior to my body so I can ignore it." As absurd as they may seem when taken out of context, such feelings can exert a powerful influence over our lives.

Try this: just watch—there's no need to fix anything. Accepting our suffering, our limitations, brings us into our bodies and opens our hearts. This is a wild state that gives us access to wisdom for our healing. We learn to listen for our inner rhythms; we learn how to cook, how to eat, from the inside out.

PART II

RHYTHMS AND RITUALS
OF THE HEARTH

THE MOUTH OF A MONK
IS LIKE AN OVEN

There is an old saying, "The mouth of a monk is like an oven." Remember this well. There is just one taste, the world itself as it is, and a simple green vegetable has the power to become the practice of the Buddha, nurturing the desire to live out the Way. Make the best use of whatever greens you have.[1]

DOGEN

ON FARMS IN CHINA AND JAPAN, the cook is often considered so valuable that he is excused from working in the fields so that he can devote his energies to cooking the midday meal. In Chinese and Japanese monasteries, cooking is regarded as an art with tremendous influence on the health and well-being of a community. Only the monks of long-standing practice and wisdom cook for the temple.

The chief cook of a Zen monastery is called a *tenzo;* the tenzo offers love and gratitude to the Buddha while preparing the meal. The preparation and consumption of food is not an end in itself, but a practice of deep religious significance. Even if the dinner is only a bowl of soup and rice, the meal can be greater than the sum of its parts.

Dogen, the thirteenth century founder of the Soto sect of Zen, wrote about the work of the tenzo, saying, "Tenzo duty is awarded only to those of manifest excellence—who exhibit deep faith in the Buddhist teachings, have a wealth of experience, and possess a righteous and benevolent heart. This is because tenzo duty involves the whole person."[2]

I used to cook with only half of my mind in the kitchen while the other half wandered freely; I knew of no other way to cook. When I moved to Hong Kong, however, my perception of kitchen work changed. I spent my first six months there as a journalist for a hotel and restaurant industry trade magazine. The job took me into hundreds of kitchens, from stainless steel and technological wonders in deluxe hotels to tiny floating restaurant boats equipped with a one-flame gas burner and a chopping block. In each kitchen, I noticed an altar. Whether on a shelf or in a wall nook, in a humble or an elaborate restaurant, the altar was tended with great care. Usually four oranges, a bowl of rice, and incense had been placed before a statue of Buddha. During festivals, the altars were filled with flowers and sweet dumplings, and some-times an entire meal was placed before the altar and later eaten.

Through my experience in China and my work in Hong Kong, I discov-ered a bridge to the inner world through the kitchen. The outer rituals made me aware of the possibility of inner attention in the midst of daily activities. A cook who uses this bridge understands the power and responsibility of prepar-ing food. Intention and attitude affects the cook, the food, and the eater.

It's not always easy to remember that the cook must "possess a righteous and benevolent heart" under the daily obligation of preparing meals and wash-ing dishes. Sometimes, just sometimes, I wonder if food pills wouldn't be eas-ier. Yet I know that whenever I weaken my intention, my health and well-being remind me how related they are to the mindfulness of my cooking.

It is a mistake to think that cooking practice requires hours in the kitchen. Practice is not about time. It's about our awareness while we cook. "In Zen, to make things sacred is to work with them. You need to put yourself into the food, and then the blessedness comes out of it," said Edward Espe Brown, Zen priest and cook for a Zen Center monastery in California. He added, "The ex-perience that comes out of opening a package of frozen foods is quite different."

When we are mindful, when we put our concentration with the food, seeing what is, rather than what we would like it to be, then it becomes nourishment. Where's your mind when you cook? Is it on the words your lover said to you at three in the morning? Is it on the dentist appointment you have tomorrow? Is it on the fact that you wished you had bought Chinese take-out instead of having to cook?

It is hard to be present. Cooking practice means we keep returning our attention to what we are doing. Then it becomes an offering. In Dogen's words, "The true bond established between ourselves and the Buddha is born of the smallest offering made with sincerity rather than some grandiose donation made without it. This is our practice as human beings."[3]

When I cook with this consciousness, it feels as if I am riding the curl of a wave that is surrounded by love. Even so, I lose my hold again and again, and forget. It's the work of at least a lifetime.

PRACTICE

Viewing cooking as a practice enables you to develop intuition and insight. It offers a break from automatic thinking and eating, and will gradually allow you to move toward the preparation of foods that will better serve you and those who eat your cooking. The following practice is one of many ways you can heighten your awareness in the kitchen.

- Today decide to approach dinnertime with no plans. You need only know what foods you have available.

- Before cooking, allow yourself five minutes to sit outside, or in a quiet part of your house. During these five minutes you will engage your intuition regarding what to cook and how to cook it.

- Tell your housemates, the children, the cat, that you are taking five minutes for yourself, and request that they do not disturb you. Initially your cat, or your child, may want to interrupt. Be kind. In time they will know this quiet period is a gift.

- Breathe deeply, with a rhythmic in-breath and out-breath, so that the in-breath is equal to the out-breath. You can count your breaths, or breathe to a specific number of heartbeats — or to a mantra. This will help you to calm down from a busy day, and assist in making the shift from active doing to receiving.

- Breathe all the way into your belly. Fill not just the belly area, but also the chest. Allow inspiration to come into you fully. Exhale the problems of the day. When you feel calm, and relaxed, then you are ready to listen.

- Close your eyes and imagine what it feels like to be taken care of, to be nourished by someone else, to be served and loved by that person. This may be difficult, but do your best. Remember a time when you felt nourished in this way. Perhaps a friend prepared a beautiful dinner for you or a child gave you a bouquet of flowers. Or maybe you treated yourself to a special meal that left you feeling full of heart.

- Once you have embraced this feeling, and tasted the love that comes through nourishment, open your eyes. If this feeling eludes you, then trust that you have begun to nourish yourself just by taking these few quiet minutes. You are making the space for nourishment, and it will come to you in time.

- With your eyes open, continue to breathe regularly, gently but deeply. Look around, and open yourself to the season, the weather, the energy of the day. Is it cool, the autumn energy dry and crackling as the leaves fall to the ground? Is the energy beginning to move down after summer's effulgence, sinking into the earth in preparation for the winter? Do you feel cold or tired? Is there a full moon or a waning moon, when energy begins to move inward? These observations will help you cook what you and your family needs. There is no need to analyze them; just allow them to drift through your mind.

- Before entering the kitchen, see if your intuition offers you a meal from the foods you have in mind. Do leftover beans transform into a bowl of creamy hot bean soup? Can you taste the freshness of a green salad to lighten up the rich heartiness of the soup?

- If, at first, ideas don't come rushing to you, trust even further in your own spontaneity and connection of heart and mind. You may even surprise yourself with your ability to play the alchemist in the kitchen.

- It's time to close this five minutes and look around you, move your body, stretch. It's time to bring the thought of nourishment into physical form.

- Acknowledge your work. You have just touched your own power and said a firm "no" to the hectic pace with which we live our lives. You have taken responsibility for your nourishment. You have risked not knowing and made room for wisdom that comes from within. The here and now of your cooking will turn into your blood, your cells, and your peace of mind.

RITUAL IN THE KITCHEN

The rituals that once conveyed an inner reality are now merely form...With respect to ritual, it must be kept alive.[1]

JOSEPH CAMPBELL

 ONE EVENING I CREATED a bedtime story for my daughters. It was about a brother and sister who lived long ago in Old Europe. Bread-baking was highly revered in their village and small loaves were often used as sacred offerings in the temples. The villagers chose the brother and sister for the high honor of a baker's apprentices. As the story unfolded, I realized that I was expressing my own need for meaning in daily life, particularly for meaning in the many chores of the kitchen.

The next time I baked bread, I changed my routine. First I cleaned out the kitchen, removing the clutter of dolls, purses, balls, old shopping lists and newspaper clippings. I lit incense and a candle, arranging them beside a vase of fresh rosemary from the garden. Then I said a blessing. My bread didn't rise higher or taste more delicious, but the sustenance I received from the clearing out of both space and mind made kneading sixteen pounds of dough a pleasure rather than a chore.

I slowly wove more ritual into my daily life. I lit a candle and said a prayer before cooking breakfast in the mornings. It felt good. I became more aware of what goes on in my kitchen. My husband Stephen and I agreed to make our kitchen sacred space. We would avoid arguments, heated discussions, talk about money or the lack of it, blaming or resentment in the kitchen.

Our lives are so often devoid of nourishing ritual. It's easy to lose our focus, to not pay attention. Listening to jarring music, talking on the telephone,

30

watching television, thinking of tomorrow while we chop and stir in the kitchen are all habits that can get in the way of the practice of cooking. Bringing ritual into the kitchen is actually a way of coming back to the center of yourself.

A Turkish Sufi teacher, while describing how to cook an egg, said to me, "All the qualities of a spiritual teacher can be found in a person who can cook an egg perfectly."[2] At the time I heard his words, my whole being strained to grasp his meaning, but it remained just beyond my understanding. Sometimes a single sentence, like this one for me, refuses to be caught. It nags and chides at the mind until one day, when we are ready, its meaning is suddenly clear. It was several years later that I realized that it is the fire in the heart that cooks the most nourishing meals. Understanding gave way to despair. It sounded too difficult. How, for instance, in the middle of a difficult relationship crisis, does one cook with love?

To raise ourselves out of the murky waters we sometimes find in daily life requires a ritual of the heart, a ritual of remembrance. For me, this ritual takes the form of a silent repetition of a mantra with each breath. I first came across a mantra while reading a book, well before I had any obvious interest in such things. It was a story about a man's spiritual journey. While in Turkey, he met a teacher who gave him the Arabic phrase, "La illaha illa 'llah." It means "There is no god but God." When I read this mantra it was like finding an old friend. I tried to stay awake that night just so I could repeat the phrase.

We can each discover our own ritual of the heart in order to cook with inner fire. But that's only the first step. The real effort is to remember. The origin of the word *forget* means to "lose one's hold." That is just what I do. I flail around until a word or phrase whispers itself to me, and then I return to the practice of remembrance. We learn to be patient with ourselves when we cook in this way.

PRACTICE

KITCHEN RITUAL TIPS

- ◆ Clean the kitchen as if it were your temple.

- ◆ Light a candle, or bring the fragrance of a bunch of fresh herbs into the kitchen. Experiment with what brings you a sense of calm.

- ◆ Notice your breathing. Is it deep with a regular, even rhythm? When I think about something else while I cook, my breath becomes shallow, going no deeper than the upper part of my chest.

- ◆ Feel your body and observe your posture. Are you relaxed, at ease in your body? Become aware of your shoulders and neck. Gently move them until you feel a release of tightness.

- ◆ Stand in the kitchen, just for a moment, without doing anything. Take inventory of your mental and emotional state. Are you feeling scattered, worried, angry? You are about to make something with your hands, and that is a power in itself. Offer up your irritability in a prayer. Don't push it away. It may be all you have to offer today.

- ◆ Limit your distractions. Your telephone is merely a tool; don't use it now. Tell a caller that you are cooking and will call back soon.

- ◆ Honor yourself as the cook. Even if dinner is leftovers and a piece of bread, respect the food and its preparation.

- ◆ Finally, free yourself from having to follow kitchen ritual. You will know when it is helpful and when it is not. It's better to keep things simple. A silent prayer may be enough.

Setting it Straight

Your intention is part of your music and never leaves it. It came from somewhere and goes somewhere. It is connected directly to your listeners and indirectly to everyone else. When the song is over, your intention keeps going.[1]

W. A. MATHIEU

ONE DAY I WAS IMPROVISING during a piano lesson. The music meandered everywhere, like whistling a mindless tune. It didn't return to its initial theme, or repeat a phrase; it just faded out. I couldn't resolve it because I didn't remember how it started. My teacher leaned over, and said quietly, "You are responsible for every note, every sound. Now play again."

This time I played sparingly, awkwardly, trying to hold purpose and beauty simultaneously. I was self-conscious, quite aware of my inability to play smoothly with this new responsibility. I went home and tried to play mindlessly again. It was no longer enough.

I now wanted structure. It would leave me free to improvise within musical boundaries and yet be supported by its form. Several obstacles kept me from learning music theory, however. The first was a dislike of discipline. The second was fear—there was something I didn't want to face. I knew this because whenever my teacher discussed theory, I could sense my consciousness dimming. I would hear his words but couldn't grasp the meaning.

This resistance to theory continued for years until I was ready to understand it. I found an old music theory book that I had used as a child; I knew that it held a clue. I put the book in front of me and inwardly asked that I be

33

shown what I needed to know. Closing my eyes, images of my childhood soon arose. I saw myself playing at a recital and was surprised by how much love I felt for music at the age of ten. The scene changed to my twelfth year. I was puzzled. I thought the clue would be found in my earlier years, but I then remembered my parents announcing that in three weeks we were leaving the United States and would not return.

Our new home was an apartment in the suburbs of Rome. My father had hepatitis and was sick for a year. He had abruptly left financial difficulties in California and the atmosphere in the house was tense. I was given a new piano teacher. She was a middle-aged woman with a dark moustache and large gaps between her teeth. Every time I played a wrong note, she slapped my hands. Within a month I decided to stop my lessons. I didn't touch the piano again for twenty-two years.

I opened my eyes and looked again at my music theory book, following my ten-year-old rounded handwriting that answered theoretical questions with ease. And, for the first time, I was able to feel the loneliness of living two decades without music. As uncomfortable as this awareness was for me, I needed to know this about myself. Only now was I able to be open to music theory.

Opening oneself to food is no different and just as difficult. It takes time to change something as intimate as our eating habits, and yet we want the switch to occur instantly. We may realize the need to eat healthier foods, closer to the rhythms of the seasons, and to the needs of our physical condition. We may long to feel nurtured, and to be able to nourish ourselves or our families with a sense of peace, without feeling haunted by a lack of time. Yet we waver and procrastinate, continuing old habits and feeling guilty for our failure. Why can't we just make up our minds and change?

There are all sorts of dramas being enacted inside of us when we want to make a change in our way of thinking, our way of being. We may re-experience being an adolescent who angrily sees discipline as a blow to developing individuality, or a child, terrified of loss. It can seem hopelessly messy when all we want to do is just nourish ourselves. We must have compassion for these parts of ourselves as well as the part that wants to change.

Try this. First, set your course. This is your intention. It draws your whole life into the picture. It steers you through choppy seas of forgetfulness until the storms calm. Intention helps us to practice, day after day. Sometimes, our intention is all we have. It walks us through periods of doubt, of frustration, of boredom, of bleakness when nothing nourishes us, and protects our longing for truth so that we don't give up.

Here is a way for you to explore intention. Think about your morning. Morning sets the mood for the entire day. The quality of the morning is sensitive to minor disruptions because of time commitments. If someone wakes up late, or forgets to buy bread the day before, or spills something at the table, then we feel the impact at this fragile hour, and this can affect how we go through the day.

Take time to consider what you most want in the morning before you start your day. Stretch beyond your comfort zone, and listen to your soul. Your ability to nourish yourself and others arises out of attention to these deeper needs. Do you want time to meditate, to pray, to walk, to sing, to watch in silence as the morning light appears, to write? Don't judge, just listen.

Before you go to bed, clear the table and set it for breakfast. This could mean table mats, spoons, cups, or a flower in a vase. Do this slowly, deliberately, consciously. You are setting the morning with your intention.

Setting the table is a hearth ritual, and there are no rules. It is a symbolic act that assists you in infusing daily life with soul. It's sacred time, even if it is just for one person. Don't fret if your intention isn't clear. Just by making the space to listen, you will, in time, hear what wants to be heard.

After trying this structure for a few nights or a whole week, begin to experiment with it. Practical considerations may arise beyond setting the table: a need to soak beans for the following day or to cook a double portion so you won't have to cook on Wednesday.

On the other hand, perhaps you are too comfortable with daily structure. Maybe it's a struggle for you to improvise in the kitchen, and you are uneasy with spontaneity. Do you plan your meals so carefully that it stops being playful? Now is the time for a pinch of wild abandon in the kitchen. Throw the manual for kitchen ritual out the window and ask yourself what needs to be born for you to be nourished. Set the table with the intention of nourishing the part of you that is hungry for wildness or beauty or humor.

This is a simple exercise, but it goes deep. It is a small step, but essential. This practice is a way of saying to yourself, as my music teacher said to me, that you are responsible for your thoughts, the sounds you make, the way you cook. Let your intention support you. Then go soak your beans.

GREETING DRAGONS RESPECTFULLY

To make things with our hands, to cook food, is a power. If you're in a bad mood, you might burn your bread. That's your energy....Understanding the power of food, the herbs and the ability to heal ourselves, is like a sacred communication.[1]

ROCKY OLGUIN

 ONE MORNING I BURNED three pieces of toast. It takes two minutes to make toast under the grill in the oven. I had put in the first piece of bread, and continued making school lunches until a burning smell alerted me to my lack of timing. I swore under my breath, and replaced the blackened bread with a fresh slice. This time the telephone rang with a change of carpool plans for that morning. I remembered the toast while on the telephone, and opened the grill to find the bread in flames. In went the third slice. By this time, the grill was so hot that the bread toasted in half the time; I hadn't factored that into my calculations. The third piece was charred by the time I opened the oven again.

It was a fair fight. The toast won. I experienced a degree of awe. It took three pieces of burnt toast to wake me up. Two weren't enough. I waved the white flag and laughed aloud. I felt as if I had landed, right there in my own kitchen, at 6:45 in the morning. What a relief it was to be back on the ground.

Morning is a delicate time of day when it is difficult to disguise our short-comings successfully. For me, it has been breakfast that has most provoked my resistance to kitchen work. It took years of kitchen practice before I learned how to greet breakfast respectfully. When the children were young, I made school lunches, snacks, and breakfast in a frenzied twenty minutes. My irritation and resentment at even being in the kitchen at such an hour was no secret. Pots banged and clanged with regularity. I was cheered on by what I came to call my dragons—those inner voices that growl. The dragons usually alert me to some imbalance in my life, often something I am afraid to address.

My old method for dealing with my dragons was to snub them as uninvited guests. I tried valiantly to disregard their presence and go on with my daily work. But I learned that the more one resists dragons, the more fierce they become. Dragons demand attention, but I had been too afraid to look. I began to wonder, however, what would happen if I listened to what they were saying. Would I abandon my responsibilities, leave my family, and run away with some beautiful wild man who survived on junk food?

Keeping the dragons out of the kitchen took tremendous energy. It was no wonder: I was trying to shut out a part of myself. Brought to the edge, no longer able to bear the tension inside of myself, I had to face them.

One day, determined to free myself of this unbearable pattern, I woke early, took a shower, and dressed. Darkness still shrouded the garden, its stillness permeating the house. I walked into the kitchen, lit a candle and a stick of Japanese incense. The smell of a Buddhist temple enveloped me and, for the first time, I prayed in the kitchen. Standing in front of the sink, I prayed because I couldn't make breakfast anymore. My years of trying to overcome my resistance to kitchen work were ended. I had failed. Finally, I surrendered.

A barrier fell away in my mind as I prayed and prepared to look deeply within. I breathed in, out, aware of my breath, waiting for the unknown. Suddenly I heard the dragons roar: "Don't waste your life making breakfast; you have better things to do! Cooking breakfast is bad for you. Your life is completely meaningless, useless. How can you do that to yourself?"

The roar eventually became a whisper, and after weeks of just listening, even though I continued to make breakfast, it finally faded out. The dragons became harmless once I paid them some attention, and they left behind a gift.

Through listening and understanding what was behind their rumbling, I realized that I had drawn and quartered my life into the practical (things I considered useful, like cooking, writing, consulting work) and the impractical (things I didn't consider useful, like playing music, meditation, and creativity.) I had put the impractical things that fed my soul into a bag that was set aside for some time in the future when I would have more time. I realized that this was like deciding not to eat because it takes too much time. I put the bag into the center of my mind, and held it there. I opened it slowly, allowing dammed up energy to flow again. I started to meditate regularly, to write and play music, and to record my dreams. It was like breathing ocean air. My blood became alive. Making breakfast was no longer a big deal. The morning dragons were quiet.

Dragons can make big trouble when we listen to them without being aware. My friend Anna listened to her dragons for years without questioning the motive behind their roaring. Every time she entered her kitchen she would hear, "You should be making money, not cooking." Her dragons caught her at her point of greatest vulnerability, her fears of inadequacy in the business world. She focused her attention on her professional success and did not nourish herself adequately. Finally, her health deteriorated into chronic fatigue syndrome.

Anna was unable to work for several years. Most of the time she had to lie on her back, unable to cook, or even think clearly. She had always relied on her energy to bounce back; this time, it didn't. Hiding behind her cynical humor was a deep grief that she later recognized as a call to dive deeper into her own being than she had ever done before. It was frightening to her; she struggled between her need for nourishment and her fear of self-knowledge.

She finally confronted the fears that had kept her from tending and honoring her inner hearth. Her recovery drew upon the strength she gained from facing her dragons.

Dragons are not predictable except in one instance. They are sure to appear when we want to make a change in our lives, in our way of thinking, or our way of being. The dragons, after all, often express our unresolved fears. When we honor the inner hearth, we can accept our dragons as well as our light. The hearth can contain the totality of these primal energies as we face ourselves with love. The destructive power of the dragons turns into our own strength to live our lives with intention.

It's the little things, even our attitude as we make breakfast, that bring us toward wholeness. When you feel ready, the next time you meet your dragons in the kitchen, greet them, and offer them a slice of toast.

The Cutting Edge

The world is as sharp as the edge of a knife.
—a Northwest Coast saying [1]

GARY SNYDER

IN THE SMALL FISHING VILLAGE IN HONG HONG where I once lived, much of the washing and chopping of food was done outside, easily visible to the passer-by. The children were expected to help, and by the time they were nine or ten years old, they were using large chopping knives. I once observed a father and his son, about ten, work together in silence. The boy carefully sliced long string beans, and then finely chopped onions. His father was chopping ginger beside him, calm and focused. The ease of the father and his trust in his son gave me the encouragement to teach my own children how to handle knives when they were still quite young.

Both children wanted to help in the kitchen at an early age. They liked to prepare food for their dolls and to help with specific dishes like a salad or dessert. For the first few years, I allowed them to use the dull dinner knives. By the time they were five or six, they were ready for a little knife education before graduating to sharper knives.

"Feel your feet on the ground, and take a few deep breaths before picking up the knife," I told them. They began with the dullest of the kitchen knives, and, in a few years, could use the larger, sharper knives. They were allowed to use these knives only when an adult was present, and the sharpest one was reserved for my use only. This worked for our children, but it is important to find out what works for yours. The child who is in the clouds, with an airy nature, and the child who is more down-to-earth will need different rules and instructions requiring knives.

I had often told Maya, our youngest daughter, that one should never rush while handling a knife, that one should pay absolute attention to cutting. One day I was cooking dinner, and Maya was sitting on the counter talking and watching me. I was moving quickly, distracted and annoyed about something else. As I chopped the raw cabbage, the knife sliced into my finger. The cut was deep and bled, and in that instant I saw the state of my mind—it had been blown around as if in a storm; it was everywhere but in the present. I tried to stop the bleeding with some paper napkins and sat down to focus on my finger. "Mommy," the voice of youthful wisdom said, "You were rushing." I smiled. The lesson had been well learned.

Breaking Patterns

Knives are an overt example of our need to be present. The impact of our lack of attention can be more obscure; this became clear to me during a period of my life when I found myself breaking cups and Chinese porcelain soup spoons by dropping them as I washed them by hand. I was able to ignore this for a time, blaming the incidences on bad luck. As the number of breakages rose, however, I had to take notice. I wanted to know what was going on. I became poised, ready for an explanation like a kingfisher waiting to dive into the water to catch a fish.

One evening as I was preparing dinner, I dropped yet another Chinese spoon. It cracked into pieces against the sink, and in the sound of breaking porcelain, inner and outer worlds met. In that moment I caught my "fish," my explanation. The split second before I dropped the spoon, a thought had flitted across my mind. It was an angry thought, spawned out of resentment.

Although I was initially stunned by what I saw in myself, I also experienced exhilaration because I was no longer at the mercy of unconscious resentments.

Self-awareness can feel devastating, particularly when we see parts of ourselves that we just don't like. Yet hidden inside this discomfort there is also a sense of wonder. While we need to be aware of how we think, how we feel, what we do, look also for that wonder. When we pay attention, life begins to express its secret to us, and we are nourished when we are on this cutting edge.

COMING HOME

Come home: To the very heart or root of a matter, closely, directly, thoroughly.[1]

OXFORD ENGLISH DICTIONARY

THE DEMANDS OF DAILY LIFE and the call of the hearth can seem irreconcilable, yet each is part of the rhythm of the day. In rhythm, the spaces between beats are as important as the beats themselves. How can we bridge the activity of our day with the nourishment we give and receive at home? The answer lies in how we negotiate the shift that occurs within us as we turn from the outer world to the inner world. It's not that being home is the inner world to which we shift. It is rather that we pause to nourish ourselves inwardly before again addressing the business of living.

Unless we respect this transition, we may, at times, feel as if we are trying to prepare dinner with a chain saw. The result is edible, but leaves us irritable. Such a meal is hardly nourishing. Just another meal, quick food, no soul.

To have time to unwind from her day's work, my friend Elizabeth takes the back roads home even though it takes longer. She is a single mother and values the evening she will spend with her son. Dinner still has to be cooked. She sometimes lies down for a half hour and reads, or, in warmer months, she takes her son to the neighborhood pool. If Elizabeth tries to cook before she has fully made the transition from work to home, it's difficult for her to make a nourishing meal. She knows that she and her son have not eaten well and feels badly about herself.

I once heard an African pre-dinner ritual. It's called "Drums for Soothing the Mind," and is traditionally played before a meal. A Ghanaian musician,

Kwaku Daddy, played it before a group of children I was with. He asked us to close our eyes while we sat, listening to the drumming. The powerful rhythms took us running across wide spaces, then into forests, crossing streams that finally led out to the ocean. When he finished, he asked the children what they "saw." "Open spaces, running, jungles, rivers!" shouted the children.

The drumming ritual works upon the mind with care. At first, mind and rhythm run together at a fast pace; impressions of the day surface. Moments later, they are released. The rhythm then becomes a stream that washes through the crevices of the mind, clearing whatever is blocked, pent-up within. When eventually the rhythm becomes slower and more even, the mind is calm, prepared to take in the nourishment of food.

Since our culture doesn't provide live drumming to soothe the mind, we must find our own rituals. One day I discovered that a hot bath while listening to Mozart did the trick. The next time it was Ray Charles. Discovering what we need in order to come home to ourselves is a mysterious combination of instinct, common sense, and grace.

PRACTICE

Here is one pre-dinner ritual that will enable you to cook with fire inside you. As you practice it over time, you will find your own rhythm with it. It will become less a ritual and more simply what you do and the way you do it.

- ◆ Water cleanses. Before entering the kitchen, take a shower and change into fresh clothes. Then take ten minutes or even a half hour for quiet time. The key is to allow the transition to take place, in its own time, slowly, gently. Stretch into it, breathe deeply into it, doing what feels right for you. Do you want to take a walk, lie down, sit in silence, listen to music? Do not listen to the radio or watch television at this time. That may only take you out again. This ritual is to help you regain your focus.

♦ No matter how rushed you are, give yourself a few minutes. If you haven't time for a shower, stand at the sink and allow water—warm in winter, cool in summer—to run over your hands. Just watch the water and listen to its sound. Just a gentle trickle.

♦ This is empty time. Nothing is supposed to happen. You do as little as possible. Sometimes you may need to start rice, beans, or some other slow-cooking dish. Knowing you have something started may help you relax. But then leave the kitchen. This is time to just be. Without a goal. This is where we may get in touch with subtle feelings that are unable to compete with daily distractions. Intuition arises from this diffuse place.

♦ Imagine that inside you is a tuning fork that vibrates at a particular frequency. In this pre-dinner ritual, allow yourself to be tuned to your own vibration, the vibration that brings you a sense of wholeness. You honor the hearth by entering into the kitchen well-tuned. Sometimes you won't be able to find this frequency. That's all right. Just listen for it, make room for it.

♦ Our technological society does not heed the rhythms of the moon, the sun, the seasons. As you relax in your pre-dinner ritual, try to identify your own internal rhythms. The rhythm of regular mealtimes is essential for growing children and supports the health of adults. Eating late at night can impose a strain on our bodies. Experiment. Discover what rhythms serve you.

◆ Let ritual come to you. If you can find just five minutes, then take them. Be patient, for invariably the telephone will ring or your child may want comforting. When you take this time for yourself, you may notice the collective pressure toward action is present. Not just outwardly, but inside yourself. You may find it difficult to give yourself this gift of doing nothing.

Whether you live alone or with others, the function of a pre-dinner ritual remains the same: it establishes a time and place where we can attune to inner and outer rhythms, pausing between the beats of our daily lives. This is a small offering we make to the hearth.

PART III

SWEEPING
THE HEARTH

ANCESTORS OF THE HEARTH

Many seeds of suffering have been handed down to us by our ancestors, our parents, and our society. We have to recognize these seeds.[1]

THICH NHAT HANH

THE DAY MY GRANDMOTHER ESTELLE DIED I held her hand and thanked her for the love she had given my daughters. She had been in a coma for days, breathing through tubes in her throat and nose. Her hair, usually perfectly coiffed even at the age of ninety-one, was thin and dishevelled. I told her I loved her, and that God loved her. Our family never talked like that, but the words came out before I could censor them. She suddenly opened her eyes. They were huge. She looked directly at me. It was glorious, like gazing into the eyes of a newborn.

Perhaps it was only seconds that she looked into me and I into her, but in those seconds there was no separation between us. Her love embraced me completely, and I sensed that this embrace included not just her love but the love of my ancestors, about whom I knew very little. Through her eyes she gave me a thread that would lead me to my ancestry; I knew I wanted to follow that thread.

Accepting our ancestry is like sweeping our hearth, clearing the ash so that the fire can burn well. If we aren't mindful of our ancestry, our nourishment is compromised. Our ancestors are a part of us; if we push them away, we reject an aspect of ourselves.

Unless we are aware, our ancestors may influence our lives without our knowledge. Shame and fear can be passed from generation to generation. These feelings may catch us off guard, triggered by a reminder of a long-forgotten memory, a phrase, or tone of voice. We can choose to explore their messages and glean their insights by paying attention to them. This is how we begin our healing. We don't have to pass these feelings on to our own children.

The positive family stories are told and retold; but other stories are buried, secret stories too painful to acknowledge. Surprisingly, these stories can be a source of nourishment.

When I first met my friend John, I was convinced that he had a secret he wasn't telling me. He laughed at the idea, but after his father had died, ten years later, he was told that his family had carried the shameful secret of a child born out of wedlock three generations ago. These days such a matter is dealt with more openly, but the unconscious pattern of secrecy and shame had affected his family for generations. When John realized that he had been influenced by his ancestors, his air of secrecy faded away.

I waited several years after my grandmother's death to open the door to my own ancestry. Even though I had written down many of the stories she had told me, I wasn't ready to pick up the thread. One has to be ready; the time must be right.

From stories gathered from both sides of my family, I soon realized that the women in my ancestry had a problem with nourishment, both the inner nourishment of the soul and the outer nourishment of food.

My grandmother Estelle's mother, Ida, hated to cook. Every Thursday, on the cook's night out, she had an asthma attack so her family would have to eat out. Photographs of Ida show a beautiful but visibly burdened woman. Her grandfather had gone to Europe for a cure for his bronchial fever and returned, months later, blind and paralyzed. He told his daughter, Ida's mother, that if she married her intended husband-to-be, he would die. And that's what he did. "When she became pregnant, he just lay down and died, and her first baby was born dead because of it," my grandmother Estelle told me.

My grandmother's words showed me that the family thought that Ida's mother was to some degree responsible for her father's and child's death. It is likely that Ida also carried the guilt passed on by her mother: this is hand-me-down guilt, held in the unconscious. Ida and her daughter Estelle had a difficult relationship. Ida died young, leaving Estelle to help raise the family. Like her mother, Estelle developed asthma and hated to cook. She became the family matriarch—powerful, with a sharp-edged humor and a love for her grandchildren. She drank whiskey daily during much of her adult life, usually politely.

I never met my paternal grandmother Pauline, although she was alive when I was a young girl. No one mentioned her name or her existence. I knew she was alive because she sent me a pair of nylon underwear every Christmas.

I didn't ask about her when I was young because I intuitively sensed that she was a forbidden topic. But when I became older, long after her death, I began to ask my parents questions about her. I discovered that for years she had lived with my grandfather only forty minutes from our house. I was told that she only wore purple in coordinated shades; hat, gloves, shoes, dress, coat, and handbag, all purple, all at once. My grandfather lost his money during the Depression, their life crumbled, and they fought regularly. She became bulimic and was treated with electric shock therapy for years. They eventually divorced, and grandmother Pauline was moved to a small hotel where she lived alone until her death. I don't know why she was so outcast; I do know that the family could not cope with the magnitude of her suffering.

I learned a great deal about myself when I heard the stories of Estelle, Ida, and Pauline. Sometimes, as in my case, our ancestors can show us more about our relationship to nourishment than our own parents. Like my grandmother and great-grandmother, I rarely cooked. I considered the kitchen a source of oppression rather than nourishment. My body finally rebelled at the lack of a balanced diet, and I became ill at the age of twenty-six. I was thrust into the kitchen for my own healing, and only then did my attitude about cooking begin to change.

On a more subtle level, I realized that I was carrying in my body the suffering of my ancestors; and that their suffering was also my own. It was only after hearing family stories that I could draw upon the richness of my ancestry. I couldn't touch the music, the passion, the strength of my ancestors, until I had also become aware of their pain.

There was no funeral for my grandmother Estelle. The evening after she died, six-year-old Maya and I said farewell in our own way. We climbed a nearby hill, bringing with us Estelle's favorites: flowers for the beauty she loved, chocolate, and a glass of wine that symbolized her whiskey. I lit a candle while Maya carefully arranged the flowers and chocolates. We sang to Estelle. We told stories about her. When we no longer needed to talk, we lay back and watched the stars in silence. We performed this simple ceremony for three years on the anniversary of her death.

When a hearth is choked with ash and buried memories, it is difficult to sustain fire. We sweep the hearth with our acceptance and understanding of what has been passed on to us from our ancestors. We do this for ourselves, our family, and for the future.

PRACTICE

◆ Many of us have reminders of our ancestors in our homes. While they may have little material value, they can carry meaning: a grandmother's tea cup, a grandfather's drawing, a great-grandmother's spoon. These objects can bring us to attention as we hold our ancestors in our heart. I put a photograph of my father's family on our mantlepiece for a few weeks. I later changed it for an old family photo of my maternal great-grandparents and relatives. It was healing just to look at their faces. A few months later, I knew it was time to put the photographs away for safe keeping.

◆ Becoming conscious of ancestral memories is a way to sweep the hearth. You may feel curiosity, boredom, sadness, irritation, discomfort. Just watch. It's not as if you think about ancestors all the time. Allow them to be on the periphery of your consciousness, coming in and out of focus, naturally, gently, so as not to push. As you become more aware, you might have dreams or insights that teach you about yourself, about what you may be carrying from previous generations. It is through your watching, your compassion, that "seeds of suffering" transform into seeds of understanding.

COAXING HABITS

Habit is habit, and not to be flung out of the window by any
man, but coaxed downstairs a step at a time.[1]

MARK TWAIN

 CROW SAT IN HIS ROCKING CHAIR; I sat on his grand-daughter's bed. There was no other furniture in the room except for an uncomfortable hardbacked chair, so this is how we always sat when I visited him. He was an old man who had suffered greatly in his life.

I must have passed by his house hundreds of times without noticing it until I came looking for him. Crow had given my husband and daughter a can of gas earlier that week when they ran out. We didn't know him, but I had a strong impulse to thank him personally. I came to his cabin with a loaf of homemade bread and identified myself. He looked blank, but then remembered my husband, and invited me in. He asked me many questions, as if he were testing the water to see if it was safe to dive in. It became clear that there was something between us that ignored generational and cultural distance. We both enjoyed ourselves. After that first meeting, Crow said to drop in whenever I felt like it.

Trust grew between us. The visits were always rich, even when we just sat together and talked about the weather. After about a year, Crow began to tell me the story of how his land—where he and other Miwok Indians had lived—was taken away by the government many years ago. His eyes filled with tears, and for the first time, he could not speak. The silence was raw. We sat together for quite awhile without speaking.

During one of my visits, Crow got up and went into a small room adjacent to the living room. It was bare except for a bed, a desk, and a few magazine photographs framed on the wall. He called me in and I watched him put a record on an old phonograph. It was a scratchy recording of Native American men chanting. I sat down on the bed and closed my eyes while listening. The sound was immediate and loud. It quickly reached a high level of intensity and remained there—no variation, no pause for breath. The noise was too big to fit into his small cabin, and I didn't think I could bear to listen anymore. Suddenly, the drumming quieted, and the chanting stopped. Crow didn't look at me. He just said, "What do you think of that?" I was shaken, and didn't want to admit it. I couldn't answer his question. He then faced me and said, "That's the trouble with you people. You don't know how to get the emotions out. When you keep them inside, it makes you sick or hurts others."

Crow died later that year. I had known him for just two years. After his death, I would go to a circle of redwood trees near my house and mourn. Not just for Crow, whose death I felt deeply, but for part of me that died when I lost the ability to feel. I had suppressed my emotions for so long that I was numb. I didn't know how to "get them out," as Crow said. Now I wanted to learn how to chant them out.

The redwoods contained me. It felt safe to release the sounds inside of me. The trees received the wildness of my grief, anger, and passion. I offered the sounds up as a prayer in honor of Crow.

Then, the land changed ownership and I could no longer go to the redwood circle. So I took the circle of trees inside of myself and found that by watching what arose within me, my emotions didn't stay "inside." The watching made them conscious and moved them into the light of awareness.

At one point I had learned that Crow drank heavily. I didn't know whether I should keep visiting him. I didn't want to support his drinking, but I didn't want to lose him either. I had decided to keep the friendship.

This experience prepared me to face my own addictive behavior. Because he had shared his pain and suffering with me, I was able to see my own. I thought I had given up my addictions in my mid-twenties. At that time my diet consisted of dairy foods, pasta, some meat, salads, wine, margaritas, and eight cups of coffee a day. I had cysts in my breasts, yeast infections, frequent colds, and dizzy spells during which I would nearly pass out. Finally I began having three-day migraines, infrequently at first, then once or twice a week. I struggled to cope, assisted by aspirin and a driving will.

One morning, on my way to work in Manhattan, I lost my vision with the typical aura that precedes a migraine. I stumbled out of the subway and knew that I had to close my eyes until the visual disturbance receded. I didn't see any benches, so I sat on a fire hydrant for half an hour with my eyes closed. No one spoke to me, although I must have been an odd sight. I didn't care. Feeling utterly ill and disoriented, I went home as soon as I could see again. That morning I resolved to do whatever it took to feel well again.

A friend introduced me to a nutritional counselor trained in traditional Oriental medicine. She showed me that the combination of foods I had chosen to eat were a primary cause of my physical condition. To begin to heal I needed to switch to whole grains, beans, fish, vegetables, seaweeds, and cooked fruits. I changed my diet overnight. I turned my back on years of old eating patterns and addictions. Within two weeks, many of my symptoms had gone. My energy level and well-being soared, and, after a few months, I felt better than I had in years.

Something was missing, however; beneath the surface of the exuberance that came with health was a sadness that wouldn't leave. I had changed my eating habits to nurture my damaged body; I was unable to nurture my innermost self. Emotions began to surface but I was unable to acknowledge them. They sank back, unwitnessed, only to resurface many years later.

After Crow died, I mourned for him and for my buried feelings. I realized that the changes we make in the interests of health may be in vain if we don't grieve for the destructive patterns we leave behind. We don't have to weep and wail, but we need to allow time for healing at the deepest levels of our being.

Permanent changing of eating habits involves the psychological and emotional levels where the habit began, as well as on the physical level where the habit currently exists. Our bodies, having grown dependent on certain foods, can react violently to abrupt dietary change. Although some people can, like I did, go cold turkey and change overnight, generally it is better to take time to change something as intimate and innate as our diet and eating habits.

One day, my friend Lauren gave up pastries, sugar, dairy, coffee, and high-fat foods. The next day her body and mind were in a severe state of withdrawal. Not wanting to believe that she could have been addicted to these foods, she ignored the early warning signals of discomfort. By mid-afternoon the following day, she experienced a desperate craving and bolted across the street to a café. In the middle of the road, she stopped, looking at the cars coming toward her, and was unable to move. Lauren felt, in that moment, that it wouldn't matter if she died. She finally forced herself to continue walking and went immediately into the café and ordered coffee and a pastry. Her rationality returned as the sugar and caffeine was absorbed into her system. She was shocked by her obvious addiction to these seemingly neutral foods. Realizing that she could be kinder to herself, Lauren began a more gradual shift from her old patterns to a new way of eating, and was now prepared for repressed emotion to surface during this time of change.

Mark Twain explained this process so simply when he wrote that a habit cannot be tossed out the window. It must be coaxed down the stairs a step at a time. If we reject something while it still lives within us, we may end up pushing it deeper into the unconscious. The roots remain.

When we coax our habits down the stairs, we allow the layers to peel away. The heart is stripped of its scar tissue, and we may touch a spot so vulnerable, so tender, it burns. Only when we can hold this burning, cradling it in our compassion, can our self-destructive patterns melt away.

THE FOOD OF DREAMS

When it is possible to hear the beloved speak himself, why listen to second-hand reports?[1]

JAMI

 DREAMS HELP US SWEEP THE HEARTH. They speak of a very real inner world that takes us beyond our self-conceptions. By listening to our dreams, we gain access to a hidden part of ourselves. We clear the hearth of old conditioning that smothers the fire.

In the unconscious, we find precious raw material for our growth—and it's not always a pretty sight. We are given a glimpse, through dreams, of the dark side of the moon—our shadow, which would be unbearable to witness in the light of day. Yet we also have those dreams that speak the poetry of our souls. These dreams call to us from such depths that we barely recognize the voice as our own.

The following is a woman's dream that hints at a longing quite unknown to her. This dream occurred many times over a period of years.

> I am at a large banquet table. My brothers, sisters, parents, uncles, and aunts are seated around the table. It is magnificently set, and waiters serve sumptuous food to all but me. I wait and wait, and everyone is served but me. My plate remains empty. I feel so much sadness, I can hardly bear it.

The dreamer did not understand the dream and ignored it. The dream first appeared while she was still in an unhappy marriage and continued through the subsequent divorce. She later developed breast cancer and had surgery.

After recovery she made changes in her life. Yet even after going into therapy, changing her diet, and starting to meditate, she still felt dissatisfied and joyless. She grew stronger, yet the dream continued to haunt her.

When she came to me for nutritional counseling, she told me about her dream and of the terrible sadness that made her so uneasy. Instead of fending off this feeling, as if it were a beast trying to bite her, she now gave it space. In doing so, a part of herself that had been buried deep within her was given permission to exist. Her longing led her to her own mystical nature that began to be expressed in her work as a painter. The dream was finally heard when she became conscious of the inner "food" that she desired and it didn't return.

It takes time to learn how to listen to dreams. The language of dreams is not the language of daily life; dreams speak in symbols. The symbols carry a powerful energy that can, at times, feel overwhelming. There is a way to meet dreams so as not to get lost in them. Ask this question: "What does this dream mean to me?" As soon as personal meaning is assigned, we have the power to look at what the dream brings. The meaning makes the dream conscious and it is that consciousness which provides protection.

Since dreams use symbols to communicate with us, they generally should not be taken literally. Yet sometimes a dream may give us an obvious insight about our daily lives. Working with the symbols can help us make changes in our way of thinking, breaking us out of fixed patterns.

Arianne came to me for nutritional and lifestyle education. She had been a vegetarian and anemic for more than ten years. This is her dream:

> I see a beautiful Native American woman walking with her arms full of food. She carries huge baskets full of corn. In her hand is a salmon, freshly caught. She is radiant, and very strong. She walks with great joy and a respect for the food she carries.

At the time of this dream, Arianne and her daughter, Tia, were both physically weak. Arianne had become so fixed in her intention to eat a specific diet related to her spiritual path that she was unable to comprehend that it could be causing their weakness. Arianne also resented her husband's dietary influence on Tia because he occasionally chose to eat fish and poultry. Food intended as a source of nourishment had created a schism in the family.

As Arianne and I discussed the dream she saw how it related to her present situation. She realized that she could trust her instincts instead of a rigid dietary plan to show her what foods would nourish herself and her family.

A week later Arianne bought some salmon. Tia was so astonished when Arianne told her the fish was dinner for the whole family that she burst out in joy to her father, "We all get to eat the same thing tonight!" she shouted happily. "We're all going to eat together!"

Within three months, Arianne's anemia was healed and Tia was much stronger. The family was able to relax when they ate, without the tension of unspoken resentments about food preferences. The dream had directly helped Arianne in her physical life and held the promise of nourishment on an inner level as well. To Arianne, the Native American woman symbolized a place within her where instincts were still intact and not suppressed by intellectual belief systems.

Once, at a dream seminar, I heard the following dream of a young woman in her early twenties:

> I am following my boyfriend on a path. He is drawn toward a range of snow-peaked mountains. I lag behind and then notice a swimming pool in a deep hollow in the earth. I leave the path, and decide to enter this pool. It is full of luxuriant flowers and plants. Inside the pool I discover an old peasant woman in the corner making a huge pancake, several feet round. It looks so delicious; I want it badly.

The dreamer understood her dream to mean that she was too busy conquering the world, so to speak, and had no time for her inner life. The dream indicated to her that she was now ready to face herself. This would nourish her in an abundant way. The giant pancake and lush growth in the pool symbolized inner nourishment to her. The peasant woman was the nurturer, Mother Earth, who could feed her with the nourishment she so badly wanted.

Dreams can point the way for us when we aren't conscious of what we want. The following dream came to a friend, Julia, who expressed disinterest in spiritual life. The dream showed otherwise.

> I am in a friend's living room. I want to peek into my friend's kitchen to see what foods she eats. I open the refrigerator and find it empty except for three loaves of homemade bread. I devour them, stuffing them into my mouth as fast as I can. I am a little embarrassed, realizing what I have done. I close the refrigerator door and open a cupboard. Hidden inside are neat piles of candy bars. I don't want these. I just want the bread.

Julia realized from this dream that she was hungry for inner nourishment. She did not want the candy that tasted good but was really only empty food. "I just want the bread," she clearly says in her dream. Julia was actually embarrassed about her own spirituality, and so it remained hidden from her. She was raised in an intellectual family where spirituality was mocked. The dream cracked her defenses, however, and allowed her longing for more meaning in life to emerge and be integrated.

Julia's dream came at a critical time; her husband had just been diagnosed with a terminal illness. He resisted her attempts to serve health foods, and eating had become a point of contention which emphasized their differences. Inspired by the dream, Julia shifted her attention from her frustration and resentment over his refusal to eat the healing foods she offered to her hunger for a nourishing inner life. She found the strength that allowed for a healing of past suffering between her and her husband. By turning within, Julia was able to love and support him in the way he most needed. Love permeated the family during the last few months of his life, allowing the children to experience the depth of their father's love for them.

Now what about the dreams that wake us up trembling in the middle of the night? The dreams we would just as soon forget because they are so disturbing? These too can nourish. Such "shadow" dreams show us what we have repressed or denied in ourselves. They may also bring up painful or forgotten memories of events in our past.

Healing is possible when what has been hidden in the darkness surfaces into the light of our awareness. Something wants our attention, and the unconscious knows how to help. Recognition of what we have repressed can free the energy that has become distorted and deformed in the darkness. It can then become a positive creative force that serves us in life.

A guide is helpful in order to enter into the dark regions of the unconscious. The guide may be a book about dream work, or a trusted teacher. Dreams follow their own laws, and we can become confused or frightened when we mistake the symbols for their literal meaning.

Even though our dreams are very personal, they sometimes need to be told. When we share the mysterious depths of ourselves with others, in a space made holy by the attitude of the listeners, then the magic of transformation can become a reality to our waking mind. Our dreams touch the dreams of the listeners, and they can provide interpretations that may help us to better understand ourselves.

PRACTICE

◆ How do we learn the way of dreams? A notebook is a good place to start. This notebook is for dreams and only dreams. Keep it beside your bed with a pen and perhaps a flashlight if you want to write down a dream in the middle of the night. Writing down dreams is a message to your unconscious. "I am listening," it says. The more you listen, the more you will remember dreams.

◆ The relationship to dreams is a delicate one that calls for respect. You can't chase after them. That would only get in the way. So just write them down. Dreams you need to remember remain with you.

◆ And yet, it may still take a long while before a dream is truly understood. Save your dream journals. One day, months or years later, reread your dreams. You might see how they warned you at times, or guided you, or revealed hidden desires. Then your dreams become old friends. This is how trust grows.

BODY RHYTHMS

Rhythm is the keeper of health, and when there is something wrong with the health, the rhythm in some way or other has gone wrong, as when the tick of the clock gets out of rhythm the clock goes too fast or too slow, and it does not give the proper time.[1]

HAZRAT INAYAT KHAN

A PHYSICIAN TOLD ME OF A PATIENT OF HERS who could no longer work because of fatigue and chronic back pain. One day this patient decided to watch her cat and do whatever the cat did. When he stretched, she stretched; when he rested, she rested; when he ate, she ate; and so it went. The cat showed her how to get in touch with her own instinctual rhythms. It was a profound lesson after which she was able to listen to her own body. She developed a growing sensitivity to the language of her body and learned how to help it heal.

It's difficult to hear the rhythms of our bodies; we so often forget and neglect it until a crisis occurs. Then, through a headache, a backache, an illness, we are forced to become conscious of our relationship to matter. How often we hear the voice of the body and then unconsciously silence it because it doesn't fit in with our schedules and our goals.

The body speaks to us in hints, intuition, and symbols. This language is different for every individual. Some hear the body through movement in dance, in gardening, in walking, in carpentry, in music; for others it is in painting, in dreams, in poetry, in singing, or in silence. This is the song of the feminine, and it calls us through matter; we hear it in our bodies. Ghanaian drummer Kwaku Daddy explains that in the Ghanaian tradition, the patron saint of rhythm is the also the patron of healing. The song of the feminine wants to be heard, and we can respond to her calls by listening and attuning to our own deepest body rhythms. These rhythms nourish and heal us.

It has, however, become increasingly difficult to accept and love our own bodies just as they are; cultural models of perfection exclude most of the population. Yet the feminine principle embraces us in our wholeness; without it we are unable to hear our own rhythms.

A client wanted to stop eating sugar because it gave her emotional swings and clouded her thinking. I suggested that instead of trying to stop eating sugar, that she try to become more aware of her body. Gradually, she would grow more sensitive and the effects of sugar would become more disagreeable to her. The desire for sugar would naturally decline. She looked at me blankly. "How do you feel your body?" she asked.

As I reflected on how I had begun to learn to listen to my body, I saw that it had not been a conscious act of waking up one morning and saying, "Now I am going to be aware of my body. Now I am going to listen to my inner rhythms." Instead, my ability to listen had arisen from my recognition of my relationship to nature.

Years ago I had read that it was a tradition among some California Native Americans to go into the redwood forests when they needed strength. Standing with their backs against a tree they would remain there until they were quite literally recharged. I remembered this brief description the day I took my husband to a hospital emergency room and watched him struggle for his life with asthma.

After leaving Stephen in the hospital, I returned home, drained of hope, and exhausted. I went to the redwoods nearby and leaned against one of the trees. Feeling soothed and calmed, I remained in this position with my eyes closed for several minutes. As I moved away from the tree, ready to go home, I noticed that my palms tingled. At about six inches from the tree, the tingling intensified, but any further away it weakened. I repeated this motion many times to convince myself that I wasn't imagining that I could feel what the Chinese refer to as *ch'i*. In Japan they call it *ki,* and in India, *prana;* we know it as the life force.

This glimpse into the unseen, which for me had previously been the unreal, gave me great comfort. I was no longer alone. I knew that I was held, a single thread within the intricate lacework connecting all living things. Before this awareness, I would have only entered into the darkness of matter, seen only the pain that is held in the body. But now I had experienced in my body the joy that is hidden in matter. It was safe for me to listen to my own rhythms.

We have rhythms upon rhythms, layered in a unique way that gives us the particular tone of our life. There are rhythmic systems within the body, in circulation, digestion, respiration, and elimination. There are the rhythms of daily life, weekly rhythms, yearly rhythms, and the much larger dimensions of the rhythms of a lifetime.

Our daughter Zoe was led to her own rhythms through a dream. She had decided to become a strict vegetarian. Her classmates had been discussing and exploring their relationships to food, and many had already chosen to eat a vegetarian diet. After nearly a month of eating in this way, Zoe became weak. She didn't understand why she was so tired and wanted to find out. Then one night, she had the following dream. "I am standing in the garden. A newspaper article appears in my hands. It says, 'Zoe should not be a vegetarian now.'"

The next day she told me the dream. She knew there was wisdom for her in the dream, and now felt free to eat what she instinctively felt like eating; she regained her strength as she returned to her own natural rhythm. The dream did not tell her that she should never be a vegetarian, but that it was important, now, to be flexible in her relationship to food. Her fatigue wasn't so much because of the change of diet, but because of the effect on her body and mind of being too rigid with her food. I had been strict with her diet when she was very young, so it was particularly important for her to break away from this pattern and trust her own intuition and instinct rather than a fixed concept in her mind.

While there are many ways to uncover our rhythms, we may stumble around in the adventure of discovering ourselves. Our conditioning and our habits can interfere with our ability to listen. I went through a long period of exhaustion when I was trying to finish a work project. I pushed myself, working long hours without breaks, and my body suffered. One day, even my mind seemed to fold under the pressure. I stopped writing, and took a walk.

When I was halfway up a hill, a red-tailed hawk landed on a telephone wire only ten feet away. We stared at each other. Intuitively I knew I should ask the hawk what I was doing wrong. The hawk didn't blink at my question; he held my gaze. And then he flew away. A clear message resounded in my mind: "When you fly, you fly. When you rest, you rest." My rhythms of working and resting were confused. I hadn't fully engaged in my work, nor did I ever fully rest without worrying about deadlines. It took me nearly a year of fatigue and backache to figure this one out. I was draining my energy by constantly overriding my own rhythms with a self-imposed schedule.

Following the hawk's wisdom, I changed my work rhythm, my energy returned, and the backache faded away. Now when I experience back pain, I know I've slipped into old patterns. When we watch for clues, the clues are attracted to our watching; it's mysterious how we discover what we need. It almost seems as if our rhythms want us just as much as we want them.

THE BROKEN HEARTH

*It seems to me that our three basic needs for food and security
and love, are so mixed and mingled and entwined that we
cannot straightly think of one without the others.*[1]

M.F.K. FISHER

 THE POWER OF FAMILY PRACTICES and their memories be-
came apparent to me during a talk I gave about the art of eating. I
asked the audience to compare their present mealtimes with childhood memories of family meals. One man said, "I was an only
child. When I sat at the table, my parents spoke of matters that I
didn't understand. I remember always thinking that I didn't even exist at the
dinner table, so I would bolt down my food as quickly as possible, rarely tast-
ing it, and then leave the table. My parents hardly noticed." He eats alone
every day now, and has done so for many years.

Another participant's parents had taught her that eating meat would "bring
the bad karma of the animal into the eater." "As a child," she said, "I tried to
eat only things with good karma so I wouldn't have to suffer the wrongdoings
of the animals." Now she lives in a women's dormitory, bringing food—
including meat—from a cafeteria to eat alone in her room. Beneath her words,
her sense of isolation and longing for a deeper form of nourishment were
palpable.

A woman from India, whose father was a politician and filmmaker, recalled meals always accompanied by political debates and disagreements. As a
child, the agitation she experienced during mealtimes interfered with her ability to digest the meal. Now, in her mid-forties, she cannot relax when she eats,
and finds it difficult to remain seated throughout an entire meal.

71

These are painful memories of the broken hearth; they are wounds. When we become conscious of the broken hearth, we can begin to heal both the pain of the past and its impact on our present lives as adults.

The hearth is held together by our focus, but this focus diffuses when old patterns or forms fall apart. Sometimes we can deal with the little cracks as they appear; these are easier to repair. There are situations of discord and darkness, however, that require every drop of our energy to maintain the focus. In these times, we can focus on what truly nourishes us, without ignoring daily reality. Inwardly we look beyond the day-to-day problems to our spiritual center, and the inner hearth becomes whole.

The family meal offers a daily opportunity to sharpen this focus. The daily rhythm of eating continues, no matter what else is happening. We sit down and eat, day after day. We know within that food, when served with love, touches us in the deepest of places, and we are nourished. We need to understand that, despite the complexity of our lives, the simplicity of focusing on the hearth allows us to take each meal, each day, and give it our fullest attention.

We can learn from the silent conversations during a meal, from the suffering not expressed or even identified. We can sense in the family's interchanges a need for less control, more spontaneity, tolerance, playfulness or harmony. All this we can learn from mealtimes.

Suzanne was a single mother of two children who managed her own business. The children spent half the week with their father who liked hot dogs, hamburgers, and chicken. The children began telling Suzanne that the food was better at Dad's house. A vegetarian, Suzanne didn't want to compromise her ideas about nutrition, but didn't want the role of "organic ogre."

As the conflict grew, so did Suzanne's resentment of the situation. After several years, the children sometimes refused to eat the "healthy" food she prepared. Meals were fraught with anxiety.

When Suzanne came to me, she was confused and angry about family mealtimes. We examined her children's behavior to see how they reflected her own attitudes, and discovered that a part of her mocked and ridiculed her own desire for healthy food. When she didn't eat well and rest, she would get sick, and then used her illness as a justification for her anger and feeling sorry for herself.

The firstborn of eight children, Suzanne received little nurturing from her mother. As a result, she didn't know how to nurture herself or her children and didn't know how to break out of the pattern. Her turning point came when she stayed with a friend during a business trip. He was a successful business owner, a single, nurturing father of two teenagers. Fascinated, Suzanne observed the way he prepared food and ate with his sons. She saw, in his natural capacity to nurture, an aspect of herself. It wasn't so much his actions, but his way of being that became a bridge to Suzanne's own nurturing abilities.

When Suzanne returned home, she became aware of negative thoughts that arose when she cooked. In time, through finding her own rhythms, she was able to nourish not only herself, but her family. She still didn't like her ex-husband's style of eating, but she no longer felt victimized by it. They began to communicate more compassionately about themselves and the needs of their children.

Suzanne can now view her cooking as creative expression rather than as a burden. She has gained confidence as she experiments with cooking meals that look good, taste good, and use healthy ingredients. Food is no longer a wedge between the children and their parents.

Ellen, the mother of a teenage daughter, married Gary, father of Kyle, an eight-year-old boy. The new couple enjoyed a well-being that they attributed to a diet high in complex carbohydrates and vegetables, and low in fat, dairy, and animal foods. Through this diet, they had experienced relief from allergies and fatigue.

When Kyle visited them every weekend, he was unhappy with the food. At home he ate what he liked—meat, dairy foods, and sugar. Kyle was asthmatic and his father explained to him that his allergies would probably improve with a change in diet. Kyle remained unconvinced and unwilling to change.

Every meal was a torment. Ellen resented Kyle's complaints and refused to cook two separate meals each time they ate. Kyle's mother accused Gary of giving the boy "food witchcraft." Kyle was caught in the middle, trying to please both parents.

Ellen soon realized that Kyle was was not the problem. She shifted from taking his complaints personally to understanding that he was very frightened. Beyond Kyle's immediate wants was a great hunger for love and security from his father and from her. Ellen invited Kyle to help cook dinners and make cookies. Ellen became more flexible, and Kyle responded to her softening attitude. She clarified her own needs and cooked only one dinner per mealtime, but with her husband, agreed to allow Kyle to make his own sandwich after dinner if he was still hungry. The mealtime atmosphere improved greatly.

The situation had seemed irreconcilable. A change took place in Ellen, however, that allowed for the possibility of something new to arise out of the family chaos. Rather than losing herself in the problems of her family, or trying to control a hopelessly uncontrollable situation, she valued what she was learning from this family story that is still unfolding. Ellen keeps returning to the love she can offer Kyle. She understands that while one meal doesn't have much impact, the accumulation of many meals is a stream of her attitudes that Kyle literally "eats." Not just in her cooking but in her way of being with the boy and his mother, Ellen contains the broken hearth in her love.

For others, childhood recollections of harmonious family mealtime rituals remain a living reality that acts as an anchor in adulthood. One woman told me that her parents learned a German blessing while living in a boarding house in Germany fifty years ago. She spoke of how visiting friends learned the blessing at her table and took it with them to their homes around the world. When she sang the blessing she could picture all the people who had shared it with her.

A ninety-year-old woman wrote to me about her childhood memory of "an important gentleman from India" who came to dinner and was so delighted with her family's simple blessing that he took it back to India, where it is still being sung by his family.

Another woman said she had taught her daughter a favorite blessing when she was six. She was deeply moved when the grown daughter visited and asked the family to sing this blessing. The daughter explained that she still found it comforting.

As a child, my friend Lee used to visit an aunt and uncle who always ended their mealtime blessing with the following words: "Shanti, Shanti, Shanti. Peace, peace, peace." Forty years later, Lee recalls how this phrase helped to carry him during his difficult childhood. Even when the meal itself was fraught with family tensions, the blessing contained him, surrounding him with safety and comfort.

PRACTICE

◆ Think back on your own childhood and how your family ate together. It is likely that this is still influencing your mealtimes. It helps to write down, in a stream of consciousness style, the memories as they come back to you. Write for five or ten minutes. Make it safe for memories to surface. Don't judge or censor yourself or these memories. This will free you to learn about your ability to nourish yourself.

- The memories may be blissful or full of anger. There may be sadness over missing something you needed when you were young. Just let the feelings flow out until they naturally subside.

- When we recognize tension that may still be living within us from the past, then we can learn to accept it, and relax. Our acceptance can't change the way things were, but as with other practices of sweeping the hearth, acceptance allows for change; it paves the way for forgiveness.

- At some point, when you are ready, visualize yourself at a meal that is the most wonderful meal you could ever imagine. You may see yourself eating with someone you love, or perhaps you prefer to be alone on a rock by the ocean. Pay attention to the sounds, the taste, the smell, and the texture, but focus on the heart of the meal. Even if you didn't experience this feeling of harmony as a child, you can allow yourself this nourishment as an adult. It is natural to want it, for it is simply daily life purified by the presence of love. When we eat, we can remember this feeling at the table.

TABLE RHYTHMS

THE MYSTERY OF EATING

*Oh wonderful, oh wonderful, oh wonderful, I am food, I am
food, I am food! I am an eater of food, I am an eater of food,
I am an eater of food!* [1]

THE UPANISHADS

 THERE IS GREAT MYSTERY in the eating of food. When we put food into our bodies, the stream of life flows through us. Educator and philosopher, Rudolf Steiner, felt that sometime in our future, eating will no longer be considered merely a physical activity but will become something consummated with soul and spirit. He wrote, "Why is it that the initiates of all ages have urged people to pray before eating? The prayer was to be an affirmation that with the food, spiritual substance enters into man."[2]

The way we eat—our conversation or our silence at the table, our way of blessing, even the attiude in which we chew our food—can become a practice that helps to repair the broken hearth. These practices, described in the following chapters, open our eyes to the possibilities of healing our relationship to the hearth and to life.

We are no longer as integrated with the world of nature as, for instance, nomadic peoples today are or our early ancestors were in the past. Once, everyday life was innately and acutely connected to the forces of nature: now, only young children seem to retain this connection.

Look at a very young child eating a piece of watermelon. Her whole body is involved. She savors the seeds, the texture, the juice—she is delighted from head to toe. No thoughts of calories, vitamins, or hazardous pesticides interfere with her watermelon rapture. She is totally absorbed in the process. Later in childhood she will develop an awareness of self, a separation from that oneness with the watermelon.

At the age of six, our daughter Maya explained to me she once thought that where she was and what she saw at that minute was all that existed. "I stood in the field, and looked at the sky, and there was nothing else, no other day and no year. Now I know there is a road, and the store, and grandma's house, summer, winter...." and she continued at length to describe her ever-expanding world.

As adults, we screen out many of the impressions that continually come to us through our senses. Finally becoming aware of something that has been there all along, we say, "That's funny, I never noticed that before." Habit, hurry, or mind chatter are a few ways we keep ourselves from being present to life.

But when we do choose to step into the mystery around us, we are never turned away. Unlike the little girl eating watermelon, we must consciously choose to participate in our experience of nature and the world around us.

When you sit down to a meal, do you ever wonder what it is that you are eating? Beyond the fiber, the fat, the taste, the crunch? We are eating life itself. Powerful forces stream down to us from the cosmos, and rise up from the earth. We draw our nourishment not only from the physical molecules of food but also from the life energy and spirit contained in food.

One day Maya was sitting at the breakfast table with a friend, cutting up pieces of French toast to save for their dolls. I asked if the dolls always ate the same food as the girls, or if they liked different food. Maya's friend replied matter-of-factly, "The dolls eat the spirit that's inside the French toast, but we eat the outside."

Physician Larry Dossey writes, "There is only one valid way, thus, to partake of the universe—whether the partaking is of food, water, the love of another, or indeed, a pill. That way is characterized by reverence—a reverence born of a felt sense of participation in the universe, of a kinship with all others and with matter."[3]

Taking meals together is a consistent way of practicing on a daily basis. The family meal holds the family heart, no matter how narrowly or broadly one defines "family." When those who consider themselves family eat together, harmony and healing within the group and within each individual can be supported. Mealtime is often the only chance we have of coming together and of sharing, not food alone, but life itself.

A recent survey reveals that among those families who dine together at home, nearly four out of ten watch televison, study, work, or read while eating. My family used to do the same. We were forced into change when my husband became ill, and discovered that eating together without these distractions is a simple but powerful practice.

Like millions of other households, our family goes through change and growth, moving out of old patterns of relating to discover more loving and truthful ways of living together. This work is not easy, but the rhythm and ritual of eating together provides a thread that can carry us through difficult times. Just as a child requires a central point from which to move outward and explore, so do adults need daily rhythm to keep us connected to each other. Like giant hands, the rhythm of eating together holds us safely when all else is in a state of flux.

At the root of many family problems is a fear of change. A family can go round and round in circles unless change is allowed to enter and heal. When a sense of peace subtly permeates a household, for even a breath, a fraction of a moment, it opens the pathway to change. We are strengthened during such times because we are forced to find meaning inwardly.

The Upanishads reminds us, "Whatever you do, make it an offering to me—the food you eat, the sacrifices you make, the help you give, even your suffering."[4] We make way for the mystery of eating by offering ourselves at the table, by becoming both the food and the eater of food.

CELEBRATION AND RITUAL

At feasts, remember that you are entertaining two guests:
body and soul. What you give to the body, you presently
lose, what you give to the soul, you keep forever.[1]

EPICTETUS

 LIVING RITUAL CAN TOUCH OUR HEARTS through our senses. It can involve taste, fragrance, singing, silence, or beauty. Breaking bread at a meal, admiring the beauty of flowers on the table, sitting for a moment's silence, or singing a simple round are ways of feeding our souls. The sense of harmony that is created when a family joins hands before a meal, or sits in silence for a moment, can influence a child throughout his life. It is the time when parents and children can step aside from daily problems and celebrate together. Rather than explaining to children about ritual, the meaning for them will grow as they grow.

Many cultures have rituals that celebrate the sharing of food. Our friend Michael introduced our family to the Jewish custom of Shabbos one Friday evening. The children listened quietly while he gave thanks for the freshly baked loaf on the table. When Michael broke off a piece of bread and, with the blessing, "Good Shabbos," fed it to one of our daughters, their eyes widened in amazement. It was hard for the children to do this in solemnity, and we were soon laughing with the relaxation this blessing gave us.

I have seen similar rituals in other cultures. In Panama, as a guest at a celebration, I watched the Kuna Indians offer their cups of *chicha,* a drink made out of fermented corn. They drank only when another villager held up his or her own cup for the other to drink. This is done with great camaraderie, and doesn't inhibit the amount they drink. The rural Quechua Indians of Peru feed the earth. They always pour some of their chicha onto the ground before drinking any of the liquid themselves. The common denominator in these blessings is that, through symbolic gesture, we acknowledge our relationship to others, and to the earth.

In ritual we step out of the way and allow grace to enter into our lives. "Establishing a pattern to our seeking is rather like cutting paths through the underbrush on our way through the forest to the river," writes theologian Sara Wenger Shenk. "We can fight our way through the underbrush to arrive infrequently at the river, or we can cut paths which lead us with relative ease to the river for refreshment, cleansing, and recreation."[2]

I was once invited to share in a twenty-minute Japanese tea ceremony with three friends. With a minimum of action, our friend served us a delicate, crumbly cookie and green, frothy tea. Except for some humorous comments, we ate and drank in silence. I consumed not just the cookies and the tea, but everything—the sound of the spring rain outside, the clarity of every twist of the wrist as my friend whisked the tea, the sharp clack of the bamboo instrument as she placed it on a tray, the texture and sweetness of the cookie, the burning taste of bitter tea, the beauty of the teapot and the moss-colored cup. How could I possibly be so full and content after eating a one-ounce cookie and drinking a half cup of liquid? Was it the calming effect of the ceremony, the loving presence of the server, the simplicity of our interactions? Yes, but perhaps most significantly, the friend who served us suggested that we not worry about correct form, only that we be comfortable and be ourselves. In this spirit of acceptance, we became full.

AROUND THE POI BOWL

Without everyday life,
it is impossible to experience silence.[1]

DAININ KATAGIRI

 WHEN SHARING OF FOOD IS APPROACHED with reverence, we are more likely to be aware of what we say or think. In Hawaii, tradition requires that only pleasant conversation be permitted around the *poi* bowl. The taro plant, the root of which is used to make poi, is the "elder brother" of the Hawaiian people. Positive conversation while eating poi is a way to honor one's ancestors.

We eat words at the table just as we eat the food. Our nervous systems soak up the conversation which, in turn, affects our digestive systems. I notice that when the conversation at the table is beyond children's experience, they become scattered and seem less nourished.

We adults are equally affected by dinnertime conversation, but we are usually less aware of our feelings and more able to control our behavior. When the conversation separates us from each other and our food, we can always choose to gently return to a subject that allows us to join with one another in the present moment of eating together. If this attitude isn't shared by others at the table, then we can still hold this space alone. Never think that honoring table rhythms just by yourself is a futile practice.

I became more conscious of table talk through silence. When our first child was just a baby, Stephen became seriously ill. Already a lean and tall man, he lost more than forty pounds in six months. The physicians agreed that he had asthma, but discovered no other reason for his deteriorating condition, and we began to search elsewhere for healing.

A nutritional healer suggested that Stephen needed to pay close attention to his diet. The healer also recommended that he eat in silence, chew well, and breathe deeply when eating. He explained that talking raises the energy in the body away from the belly and reduces the energy available for digesting and assimilating food. Eating in silence was a gentle way to re-establish Stephen's natural rhythm. We agreed to give it a try.

The first week of silent meals was almost unbearable for me. I had never eaten in silence, and I felt awkward and isolated. I watched anger arise in me; it came from the thought that my freedom was compromised by eating in silence. Although it was always easy for me to be alone in silence, I found sharing silence with another person painful. While I couldn't ignore the feelings, I chose to be with the silence. For the next few months, dinner sounds consisted of the baby's babbles and my responses to her. After dinner, we would talk over tea. Finally, Stephen began regaining energy and weight, and, to my relief, we began to talk during the meal.

A strange thing had happened. Unknown to us, we had become sensitized to the silence. When we brought up the topics we once had discussed over dinner, like money, work crises or daily or global problems, it was disruptive. It felt like sandpaper on tender skin, yet I didn't want to return to imposed silence. Although therapeutic in one sense, silence was neither a practical nor nourishing way to live with a growing family.

Together we decided to leave negativity behind as we sat at the table. Not that we always managed to do this, but the mutual agreement held the space as we became more aware of our conversation. If we fell into silence, it was a natural, easy silence.

I later found that silence can be shared with children. One evening, I felt irritable and stressed and had a strong need for a quiet dinner. I was alone with our two healthy and rowdy girls and wondered how I could handle their noise.

I suggested that we see who could be quiet for the longest time. To my surprise, the girls were excited by this new game.

Initially they were wild, trying to make one another laugh by making faces and using sign language. In a few minutes, however, they quieted, and the atmosphere changed. The meal took on a very special quality. Although the silence lasted no more than five minutes, it was enough. I felt us connect to something beyond ourselves, and a delicious sweetness lingered for the rest of the meal. The girls became attentive, and seemed happier and more centered. I never initiated this game again, but the girls did. They could sense their own need to bathe in silence, even if it was only for a minute.

In some parts of the world, eating in silence is the custom. A Portuguese woman told me that when she was a child, her large family always ate in silence. It was after eating, over coffee, that the table became lively and animated. I have since heard of other cultures where people eat quietly and then sit around the table for conversation.

Silence in our culture makes people uneasy at first. Silence should never be imposed on others. At a Zen monastery in California, one of the Zen teachers explained to me that they used to request meals be taken in complete silence. People were so uncomfortable, wondering how they should behave, where they should rest their eyes while chewing, what other people thought of them, that the silence created more tension than calm, and some visitors complained. So the monastery compromised. Now there is a short silence only at the beginning of the meal; then people talk if they wish.

Silence is powerful; it must be approached with sensitivity. There are times when silence during a meal may be important, while at other times it may be a hindrance. Silence at meals is interesting to explore; many find it increases the energy obtained from the meal. But beware. A little silence in a noisy culture is revolutionary; you may learn to love it. If that happens, share your silence with those who also love silence.

CHEWING PRACTICE

In silence, O dear one, eat without haste. With peace, delight, and one-pointedness, thoroughly chew your food. Don't eat merely for the pleasure of taste.[1]

SWAMI MUKTANANDA

HOW TO EAT IS NOT A NEW SUBJECT. In the Essene Gospel of Peace, Jesus instructed his followers on how to eat:

And when you eat, have above you the angel of air, and below you the angel of water. Breathe long and deeply at all your meals, that the angel of air may bless your repasts. And chew well your food with your teeth, that it may become water, and that the angel of water may turn into blood in your body. And eat slowly, as if it were a prayer you make to the lord. For I tell you truly, the power of God enters into you, if you eat after this manner at his table.[2]

Just as the ritual of silence is common in some cultures, the American culture also encouraged eating slowly and thoroughly up until World War I. Now our language is rich in descriptions that attest to our desire for speedy eating: fast food, gulp it down, grab a bite, eat and run. Eating has become hazardous. Choking on unchewed chunks of food is a common cause of accidental death in the United States. Statisticians call it "death by food inhalation." Many of our grandparents were taught to chew each bite as many as thirty times; they knew the wisdom of chewing.

Noboru Muramoto, teacher of traditional Oriental healing, explains the importance of chewing. "Healing power, a strong immune system, and body rejuvenation are all enhanced by good chewing...Chewing is not a subject that satisfies intellectual curiosity; it is a matter of practice."[3]

Thorough chewing requires deliberateness, focus, and attention; when approached in this manner, it can be a meditative act. It can also be, of course, commonplace and boring. I once had a dream in which I saw what seemed to be the props for a still life painting—a vase of flowers, a bowl of fruit, and a pitcher of water. I thought, "How dull, how ordinary." Then a voice said, "You must turn this into beauty by the way you look at it." The objects then began to shimmer and radiate exquisite colors and light. As in my dream, we can choose to see chewing, just like every action in our daily lives, as ordinary—or perhaps not.

During a lecture about the art of eating, I once asked a roomful of fifty people to chew a piece of bread until it became liquid in their mouths. Everyone closed their eyes and chewed with concentration, generating the sound of a peaceful, swishing stream. At first I watched, but then closed my eyes because I felt as if I were intruding upon something very private. As I sat, I could feel the energy in the room change from self-conscious embarrassment to complete calm and peace.

When I asked for responses, a reserved man shared his surprise that he felt connected to his heart while eating. He hadn't realized that such a connection was possible between conscious eating and the heart. A woman described how full and complete she felt after that one bite and wondered if, in the future, she would not need to eat so much if she chewed more thoroughly. Another person described feeling calm, and one man said that he felt as if he were remembering something he had long ago forgotten.

I have found that the busier I become, the less I want to chew. I grow impatient, and eat faster. Slowing down, breathing deeply, and concentrating on what I am eating forces me to pay attention. Eating in this way brings me back to my body when I have forgotten about it.

According to a study conducted at Temple University in Philadelphia, students who meditated while eating digested their oat cereal much more efficiently than those who were asked to perform mental arithmetic during the meal. This study found that relaxation not only produces more saliva, but also raises enzyme levels which improve the body's ability to digest carbohydrates. Tension reduces the production of saliva, making digestion more difficult.

Yogic philosophy holds that the prana, or life energy, contained in food can be absorbed by the nerves of the tongue, mouth, and teeth. The act of chewing liberates this prana, which can then be conveyed to different parts of the nervous system. From there, it is distributed to all parts of the body, furnishing energy and vitality to every cell.

Find out for yourself what works for you. But I suggest you go far beyond chewing. Eating can be prayer. Jewish mystic, Michel Abehsera, hints at this prayer when he describes a Sabbath meal in which he prepares *cholent,* a dish cooked for eighteen hours:

> You have to come ready for this type of dish. It will be hard to digest if you are not happy. I am not speaking of usual happiness, the one which arises from one's own nature. This has its own limits. I mean the kind of happiness that Heaven commands one to have. This one is a deed, a great catalyst that has you transmuting stone into baby cream and nightshade food into dance. A Sabbath meal and the happiness that accompanies it, the chants, the singing, the light, touch a place in the memory which gives vigor to the entire being. Eden is only a breath away. You are made king by law. At last you reach your real dimension.[4]

PRACTICE

◆ Choose a time when you won't be distracted, and a quiet spot where you will eat your meal. Give the food your undivided attention. This is a slice of unmarked time in your daily life. Nothing else goes on except eating. Watch out, for the mind is uncomfortable with such stillness. It will want to think about some pressing problem, or reread the cereal box. The mind's incessant song may tell you that you shouldn't take time like this for yourself. Tell it to go fly a kite while you eat in peace.

BLESSINGS

The head of the household always sits down and gets served first, especially when he is a holy man, like my grandfather was. He might say a prayer before starting to eat, or he might ask someone else to say it, especially if there was someone whose prayers were noted for strength. But since they prayed all day long anyway, they didn't necessarily pray before each meal. Nowadays I hear more praying at meals, but less at other times.[1]

BEVERLY HUNGRY WOLF

 ONE DAY, OUR DAUGHTER returned home from kindergarten with a blessing that she sang for us before we ate. She delighted in thanking the wind, the rain, the earth, and the sun for the food we were about to eat. It sounded sweet from her, but I was uncomfortable with singing it myself; I didn't grow up with any form of grace before meals. I was willing to try, however, seeing the pleasure it gave her.

Initially it felt artificial, but the dinner blessing soon became a welcome part of the day. In order to eat together, we yield our personal schedules and set aside our separate lives to unite around the table. Eating alone is no different; if we take even a few seconds to breathe deeply and come back to ourselves, we are aligning with the unity rather than the fragmentation in our lives.

Just as in cooking, however, it's not the ritual itself that transforms a meal. Zen Master Dogen put it this way: "Don't cook with ordinary mind and don't cook with ordinary eyes."[2] Although he is talking about how to cook, he is also talking about how to eat and how to live.

Routine puts us to sleep, and it becomes all too easy to eat with ordinary mind, ordinary eyes. Yet the rhythm of a blessing before we eat provides an empty space that invites and invokes our gratitude for creation.

It takes time to become comfortable with the intimacy of this space. Allow yourself to be uncertain, to experiment with finding your own way of blessing. A blessing doesn't have to be traditional, nor does it have to sound "holy." You may want to make up your own, or choose silence insead of song. For some, including myself, it can take a long time before the hidden part that knows what to do in this emptiness becomes conscious. For others, especially children, singing praise is as natural as breathing. Here are a few blessings from different traditions for you to explore, if you don't already have one of your own.

ARAPAHO PRAYER BEFORE EATING

Our Father, hear us, and our Grandfather. I mention all those
that shine, the yellow day, the good wind, the good timber, and
the good earth.

All the animals, listen to me under the ground. Animals above
ground, and water animals, listen to me. We shall eat your
remnants of food. Let them be good.

Let there be long breath and long life. Let the people increase,
the children of all ages, the girls and the boys, the men of all
ages, and the women, the old men of all ages, and the old women.
The food will give us strength whenever the sun runs.

Listen to us, Father, Grandfather. We ask thought, heart, love,
happiness. We are going to eat.[3]

BLESSINGS

THANK YOU

Thank you for the trees that grow,
Thank you for the flowers,
Thank you for the soil below,
Thank you for rain showers.

Thank you for the flame that glows,
Thank you for the wind that blows,
Thank you for the Earth we love,
Thank you for the sky above.
    Maya, age six

SANSKRIT BLESSING

Praise the food served to you,
Never criticize it.
Food is Brahman.
Food is the Self.[4]

THE THREE TREASURES

We venerate all the past teachers
and give thanks for this food,
the work of many people
and the offering of other forms of life.[5]

AMAZING GRACE

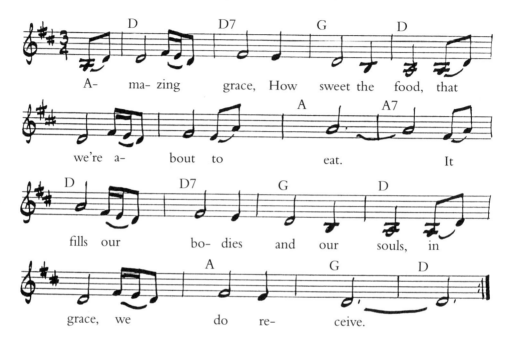

A- ma- zing grace, How sweet the food, that

we're a- bout to eat. It

fills our bo- dies and our souls, in

grace, we do re- ceive.

ROUND

For thy gra- cious bless- ing, For thy wond rous word,

For thy lo ving kind- ness, we give thanks O Lord.

GIVE THANKS (ROUND)

Give thanks to the Mother   Gai-a, Give thanks to the Father Sun, Give

thanks to the beauti-ful garden where the Mother and Father are one. Give

thanks, give   thanks, and to   you we   do give   thanks. Give

thanks, give   thanks, and to   you we do give   thanks.

CANONIC GRACE

FOUR PART ROUND

Oh   Thou the sustainer of our bodies hearts and souls bless all, bless all.   That

we re- ceive in   thankful -ness, A- men,   A-   men.

PART V

EARTH RHYTHMS

THE FIVE PHASES

O World, I am in tune with
every note of thy great harmony.
For me nothing is early, nothing late
if it be timely for thee. O Nature,
all that thy seasons yield is fruit
for me. From thee, and in
thee, and to thee are all things.[1]

MARCUS AURELIUS

 IN A DREAM, I ASK A FRIEND who is a Greek scholar, "What is the Goddess?" He then presents me with a twelve-foot calendar of the Goddess. The calendar is magnificent, and although I cannot see it clearly, I sense that each month is drawn artistically, with the dates below it. I understand from this calender that I can experience the sacred in matter through day-to-day participation in the seasons.

The seasons are a mysterious gift from the sun, each season offering us its special charm and beckoning us to intimacy with the earth. The movement from season to season is natural, constant, and, like all change, inevitable. Attuning to and participating in each season provides us with insights into our own patterns of change.

We must reconnect with the slower rhythms of nature as we tend the hearth. Respect for the rhythms of nature allows us to respect the natural rhythms of the inner world. When we are in tune with these rhythms, we can work in harmony with ourselves. "Nature is without and within us, each of us every moment," writes Diane Connelly, doctor of traditional Chinese medicine. "We are a replica of the universe passing from season to season in a natural unending cycle of life."[2]

The Chinese theory of the Five Elements, sometimes called the Five Phases, is a model of the annual cycles of nature that reveals our relationship to the earth. The European tradition uses four elements: Earth, Water, Air, and Fire. The Chinese system has five: Wood, Fire, Earth, Metal, and Water.

I prefer to use the term phases rather than elements because they are not fixed states, but are constantly transforming. The fullness of Fire, in the summer, moves into the transitional phase of Earth or late summer. Earth becomes the more contracted phase of Metal (autumn) that contracts even further to become the Water phase, winter. The abundance of summer has now transformed into the emptiness of winter. This emptiness begins to expand and fill until we see the activity and growth of spring, the Wood phase. And the activity of spring increases to become the full expansion of summer.

The naming of the seasons or the phases, is a way to become conscious of the constant state of flux in nature. Naming, however, creates separation for we must stand apart from a season in order to name it. Yet the naming is the key that allows us to consciously participate in the experience of the seasons.

Growing children also move toward the fullness of consciousness as they leave behind the period of childhood when they simply flowed from day to day. Like adults, they relate their memories to the seasons: a night walk in spring or an unusual snowfall on Valentine's Day. These are reference points that give us our bearings, establishing our physical presence on the earth.

The phases explain the interplay of five forces, reflected both in the outer macrocosm and inner microcosm of our bodies. Each phase is associated with a season, a body organ, and an emotion. Disorders are described as an excess or deficiency of one phase, disturbing the flow of the other phases. All five phases reside within us. Using this model of nature can help us correlate the physical changes of nature with the experience of our inner seasons.

Eating seasonally helps us to harmonize with the different seasons. Cooking styles, too, vary with seasonal changes. We already know instinctively that we want to eat more lightly in summer, with more fresh salads and raw fruit, while we naturally want heartier foods in winter. When we understand the subtle shifts as we move from phase to phase, we develop keen intuition about our daily food.

In the ancient text of *The Yellow Emperor's Classic of Internal Medicine,* the five phases are described in this way: "The interaction of the five elements brings harmony and everything is in order. At the end of one year the sun has completed its course and starts anew with the first season, which is the beginning of Spring. This system is comparable to a ring which has no beginning nor end."[3]

So enter consciously into the ring that has no beginning or end. Live with awareness of the rhythms of the seasons; touch them with your bare hands. The changes of nature are food for the soul. Now, take a moment, breathe deeply, and experience this season. Let the season touch you inside.

Spring

SPRING IS THE DIVINE KISS. I watch the apple orchards burst into full blossom, and I want to capture this exultation, hold it, savor it. It's only a matter of days before the blossoms scatter in the wind and the trees return to being ordinary apple trees.

The transition from winter to spring provides the perfect opportunity to explore the inner workings of nature. Toward the end of winter, when nature still appears to be asleep, an unseen, energetic shift takes place. In its own time, it breaks through into the world we see. Bulbs, buds, wildflowers and grasses emerge from beneath the earth, affirming once again the tremendous regenerating force of nature.

This transformation from death to life, this time of new growth, of potential not yet realized, brings changes in our own internal landscape. Although the spring equinox occurs on March 21 when the length of day and night are equal, the motion toward spring actually begins many weeks before this date. The Chinese solar calendar marks a time, several weeks before the equinox, with a festival called Awakening Insects. It corresponds with an increase in flies and mosquitoes and the first sounds of frogs and cicadas, revealing the stirrings of nature. Women pray for fertility of the fields and for themselves, linking the new growth of nature to their own potential for conceiving.[1]

Many spiritual traditions of the world emphasize the importance of eating simply or fasting in spring. Lent, the forty days extending from Ash Wednesday to Easter, has been observed with fasting for centuries. On Shrove Tuesday, the day before the fast begins, many Lenten observers used to consume meat, butter, sausages, fats, or other rich foods which they would abstain from eating for the next six weeks. Today, in some cultures, special pancakes made from many of the soon-to-be forbidden ingredients provide a special treat; other cultures celebrate Shrove Tuesday with Carnival or Mardi Gras (literally "Fat Tuesday" in French) as a last fling before the long Lenten fast.

Changing our daily diet in anticipation of spring assists the healing of wintertime ills and prepares us for spring's exuberant flow of energy. It's difficult to invite growth and new beginnings when we are laden with the heavy, heat-generating foods of winter.

The cleansing we offer our bodies in spring strengthens our internal organs for the entire year by helping to dissolve stored fat and mucus. The heavier winter foods may present our organs with too large a daily load of waste matter, causing difficulty in toxin elimination. The organs then become clogged and stressed. A simple and safe antidote is to prepare foods that have a lighter quality than our winter diet, omitting or reducing our intake of high-fat items such as dairy foods and animal protein.

The powerful rising energy of spring clears obstacles on the cellular level and in our minds and emotions, creating a greater sense of flexibility and clarity. Spring lightens us up, allowing us to move forward without last year's extra luggage and preparing us for the heat and activity of summer. In the Five Phases, spring is associated with Wood. The Wood phase governs the liver and gall bladder which are most active in spring. Like spring itself, the liver has a remarkable regenerative ability.

The liver is the body's largest internal organ, a filter for our blood. Overeating or inappropriate diets, especially fats, alcohol, caffeine, sugar, and chemically processed foods overwork and tax the liver. For regeneration we don't have to avoid these foods completely, but making a change in our eating patterns is essential. Such a break provides an opportunity to separate habitual eating from our actual needs.

Eating plenty of vegetables and including cleansing herbs as teas assist in the spring lightening-up process. Many herbal teas such as red clover, nettle, and burdock can be used to cleanse and strengthen the body. Nettles grow abundantly where I live, so I collect the young leaves and drink nettle tea daily for about a month in spring. Even the children like its mild taste.

I begin to lighten up my cooking in late winter, moving into the energy of spring about a month before the spring equinox. By doing this, I avoid a tendency toward congestion and colds. I prepare clean-tasting meals, using less salt and oil than in winter. The foods that grow during this season contain spring's rising energy and are good to include in the diet. Wheat, oats, and rye can be included for their Wood-like energy. Sprouts, scallions, and leafy greens help cleanse and lighten the body. Herbs such as fennel, rosemary, parsley, and chive enliven dishes and help the body to respond easily to spring's strong upward energy. Wild greens such as dandelion and nettles can be cooked and eaten just like vegetables. They have been used traditionally in parts of Europe and North America because of their potent blood cleansing properties.

If you don't have access to wild foods, you can still use lightly cooked green vegetables for a similar effect. Buy seasonal greens that can be found in any supermarket and eat them for breakfast to supplement your toast or hot cereal. Sprinkle with a few drops of lemon juice if you like a sour flavor. Having spent much of my life in Asia, eating vegetables for breakfast no longer seems strange. Try it for a few days and notice how you feel by mid-morning. It's a great boost for your liver, and indeed, for the whole system. Buy vibrant, organically grown greens if possible. You'll notice the difference.

The Chinese Five Phase theory associates the sour flavor with springtime. A little sour taste stimulates the liver, but too much can cause damage. A little lemon in salad dressings, some mild rice vinegar or other types of natural vinegars might feel cleansing to your system.

The sour flavor is also found in pickled vegetables. Sauerkraut, for instance, stimulates digestion and supports the detoxifying function of the liver. The lactic acid in fermented foods protects against infection because it can help stop the growth of bacteria and works against putrefaction.[2] If you suffer from heart or kidney weakness, be cautious with your salt intake.

As the weather grows warmer, our diet also adapts to the new season. I begin to include green salads in spring, but while the mornings are still cool, I'm not attracted to eating too much raw food. Root vegetables, like carrots, grow deep in the ground and have a strong stabilizing energy. Grated, they complement the lighter energy of leafy salad greens. Another root, the long white radish known as daikon, is known in Japan as a vegetable that helps dissolve fat in the body, and is particularly beneficial in spring.

Beyond the spring-like foods we take into our bodies, we bring spring into our souls through celebration. One of our family's favorites is to make an egg tree, an old tradition in many parts of Europe. The eggs and the new growth on the branches symbolize the inner meaning of spring. By making an egg tree, we touch with our hands the outer beauty of these inner symbols.

Here's how: find a large branch with young green buds or blossoms on it, and set it in a plant pot filled with small rocks or soil. Eggs are "blown" by puncturing a pinhole in each end of the egg and blowing out the contents. Paint the dried, clean eggshells and hang them with thread or ribbon onto the bare branches. The best shells are saved while new ones are added each year.

SUMMER

THE SUMMER SOLSTICE OCCURS ON JUNE 21 when the sun reaches its highest glory. Summer's energy is very active, but also marks the beginning of movement toward the winter solstice. In ancient Britain and Europe, summer solstice was a fire festival of great importance; the sun was thought to be ritually strengthened by bonfires burning on Midsummer's Eve. These fires were lit to give magical aid to the sun which, in the full tide of summer, begins to wane. People danced around the fires on hills and in villages, and on St. John's Eve in England, a few days after the solstice, young men leapt through flames as a purifying and strengthening rite.[1]

In the Chinese Five Phase theory, summer is the most expanded stage of the seasonal cycle and is associated with the element Fire. Summer represents functions that have reached a maximum state of activity and are about to decline. The Fire Phase governs the heart and small intestine, and is associated with the two meridians, or pathways of energy, in the body that relate to circulation and heating. The flavor linked with the Fire phase is bitter.

In the temperate zones, hot, dry weather encourages vegetables and fruits to grow quickly and abundantly, with a high water content. Juicy watermelons, cucumbers, lettuces, tomatoes, summer squashes, and other summer foods provide a cooling aspect to our diet. Corn, although classified as having a Fire energy, is light and easily digested in summer. The bitter flavor associated with this phase is in watercress, chicory, some varieties of lettuce, parsley, and dill.

Summer herbs are light and refreshing and aid assimilation. The various mints, as well as marjoram, thyme, rosemary, and summer savory, calm and refresh us, soothing the digestive processes.

We must be careful to tend our digestive fire in the summer. If we have a weak Fire energy, that is, if our digestive system is not working efficiently, then it's far too taxing on the digestive system to eat only cold foods during the summer months. When autumn comes, we wouldn't be able to generate sufficient warmth to keep our systems functioning harmoniously. Some of the symptoms that indicate one should stay away from too many raw or cold foods are: feeling cold easily, particularly in the autumn and winter; poor digestion, with a tendency to flatulence; and weakness in elimination.

Steamed or lightly boiled vegetables cool without dampening the fire. Once cooled, arrange them on a bed of lettuce with dressing. Cooking transforms the energetic quality of the salad, transforming it from cold to gently cooling.

Pressed or lightly pickled salads, common in Asia and parts of Europe, stimulate the appetite and aid digestion during the summer months. Gently mix a thinly sliced head of lettuce or Chinese cabbage, sliced red radish and red onion, and a small pinch of salt in a bowl. Place a weighted plate on the salad for an hour. Discard the liquid that has accumulated and season the salad with a dressing or add a little lemon juice or rice vinegar. A pressed salad makes a refreshing side dish and is particularly suited to those who eat a grain-based diet. Meat eaters usually prefer raw salads which are a more suitable balance for their systems.

When I traveled through Asia and Central America, I discovered that these cultures consider cold foods and drinks to be weakening to the stomach and spleen. In Hong Kong, I frequently ate lunch with my Chinese co-workers, who, like others in their culture, did not indulge in iced drinks. As I began to drink my iced tea one day, my friend clucked at me, saying that was "no good." In answer to my question why, he told me that "it makes you too cold." Behind the simplicity of his comment lie three thousand years of traditional wisdom.

Admittedly, the diet of industrialized countries has changed from ancient times and typically includes a much higher percentage of protein, fat, and meat than ever before. Consequently, iced drinks and cold food help to cool down the excessive heat generated by such a diet. Yet our bodies have limited tolerance for an excess of cold foods over a long period of time.

In summer we have a choice before us. We can cool our systems by frequent consumption of frozen snacks, icy drinks, or food straight from the refrigerator. For a more gentle approach, we can keep cool by eating cooling foods, such as vegetables, fruits, and salads. Then, on those unbearably hot days, iced drinks and frozen desserts become wonderful treats.

Joy is the emotion associated with the Fire phase.[2] While this is the most dynamic state of the Five phases, it is, paradoxically, through its opposite—inactivity—that we feel the interior fullness of summer. Filled with summer's Fire, we are then ready for the following seasons. This means opening to summer by taking time apart from our typical summer activities to sit by a lake and watch the changing colors at dawn, hike in the silence of wilderness, or lie in a city park with no goal in mind. In this way, summer embraces us. The embrace is full, ripe, fruity, and its joy is a quiet one.

Late Summer

Just before the edge of one season meets the next, there is a magical no-man's land—a transitional time, an invisible shift. This is the Earth phase, moving toward the consolidating, grounding forces of autumn and winter. The shift occurs after the full peak of growth has passed, and signifies the beginning of harvest time. This season is deceptive because the temperature may still be hot and summery. We can be fooled into thinking we can continue with the same pace and diet as summer.

The Earth phase has a dual nature, representing not only the time between summer and autumn, but also the transition between each season. As with any change, it's important to stay grounded. Unless we are centered, we may be thrown off balance in the midst of energetic changes.

When we eat, we can shift from a lighter summer diet to foods that provide warmth and energy. We need to build and tone our bodies for winter by adding more warming foods to our daily diet. Even though it may still be hot outside, it's wise to follow the energy of the season, not just the temperature.

I like to go to a farmer's market and explore the delight of seasonal vegetables. In late summer, sweet vegetables such as squashes and onions abound. These vegetables touch the earth's surface while they grow and have a calming effect on the body. Mid-summer vegetables seem to expand upwards and outwards in the hot sun. In late summer, however, the energy begins to come back down to the earth, and the vegetables hug the earth at this time. Later, in colder months, the root vegetables descend even deeper into the earth.

The flavor for this season is sweet, according to the Five Phase theory. This is the sweetness of golden squashes, baked apples, grapes, carrots, onions, and grains such as millet. Prepare sweet root vegetables such as carrots more lightly than in winter by lightly boiling or steaming them until just tender, allowing them to cool, and adding them to a green salad. We can increase our intake of root vegetables in this season, yet combine them with raw foods while the weather is still hot.

The organs associated with the Earth phase are the spleen, stomach, and pancreas. Our digestive system is sensitive to our emotions, and functions best when we are centered. The emotion linked with the Earth phase is sympathy or compassion. To express compassion, we must feel grounded within ourselves, otherwise we may get lost in the problems of others. An imbalance in the Earth phase expresses itself as anxiety, instability, and a feeling of not being connected.

Late summer is a pivotal time, and quite specifically brings us to the hearth, the center. Here is a way to attune yourself to the Earth phase: imagine yourself poised between summer and autumn. Become aware of any changes you feel internally or externally, knowing that this is a time of transition. Just as the vegetables hug the earth at this season, be attentive to what makes you feel grounded. Look for the center that does not change.

AUTUMN

EVERY AUTUMN, I usually manage to cajole the family into taking a hike together. This is often a busy time and walking together slows us down so that we can experience the season. I love hiking to the Pomo Canyon in Northern California. It's heavily wooded with bay trees, oaks, and madrone, making it cool and dark as we follow the path uphill. Just when the girls ask "how much longer?" we abruptly walk out into bright sun as the terrain changes to open grassland. We continue to climb for another half hour and finally reach the top ridge. The Pacific is now in full view as we eat our lunch. Oak leaves make a dry, whispery sound as the wind blows through them, and the girls collect fallen acorns. It's our annual autumn ritual.

During autumn, the earth seems to inhale, to breathe in, its energy drawn downward. In our garden, I notice the life of the onions has moved back into the bulbs, leaving the stalks brown and withered. The cucumbers have stopped producing their juicy fruits, and the vines have turned hard and dry, lying lifeless on the soil.

This is the Metal phase, representing functions in a declining state. It is the most contracted energy of all the seasons; a time of gathering together; a time to prepare inwardly for winter, releasing old patterns, letting them naturally dry up and blow away in the autumn wind.

The fall equinox occurs around September 21, but the easing of late summer into autumn is not so clear-cut. The energy shifts gradually until one day we wake up and we know it's autumn. Harvest time provides a consolidating energy that helps us get our work done and prepare for winter, in both outward and inner ways.

African drummer Kwaku Daddy says that drummers in his village play a rhythm called *disinkro* during the fall harvest. The beat seems to assist the workers, easing their backs. As I listened to his drumming, I could feel that sense of intention and strength that occurs during harvest time.

According to traditional Chinese medicine, the lungs and the large intestine become more vulnerable during this time of year. The nose, known as the entry point into the lungs, may become congested, and people are more susceptible to coughs. The large intestines are stimulated during autumn, and appetites wake up as well. But if too much food is eaten, the large intestines can become weakened, with an accompanying weakening of the lungs.

Sadness or melancholy is the emotion associated with the Metal phase. A weakening of either the large intestines or the lungs can therefore result in depression. It also works in the other direction: a prolonged period of grief or sadness can weaken the lungs. We can use creative expression throughout the year in the form of artwork, writing, or music as a container for our emotions so we don't hold them inside.

The pungent flavor, associated with the Metal phase stimulates the large intestines and the lungs, assisting in breaking through any congestion. This flavor can be obtained through horseradish, sharp-tasting mustard, sliced green onions, mustard greens, radishes, and grated ginger. In moderation, this flavor warms and clears, whetting our appetite and assisting in digestion. While many adults relish pungency, this flavor may be too sharp for most children.

When the temperature drops, I begin to cook heartier dishes, with an emphasis on stews and thick soups. Our family enjoys the return to these stronger, more invigorating dishes, especially the one-pot meals: vegetable or fish stew, or a rich soup of beans and vegetables. Everyone helps themselves from a large pot in the middle of the table. A separate pot of rice (the Metal phase grain) combines well with such a meal.

Vegetables cooked for a relatively long period of time carry a strengthening quality, warming us more than foods that are lightly cooked. Root stews are particularly strengthening, with large chunks of carrots, onions, and squash for a rich flavor. Balanced with a light salad, or boiled autumn greens topped with a dressing, and perhaps a slice of whole-grain bread, the meal is complete.

Leafy green vegetables, like the seasonal kale, collards, mustard greens, and Chinese greens, serve to promote rhythmic activity in our lungs and to cleanse our blood. The darker greens contain strengthening minerals including large amounts of calcium.

"Greens again?" say our children, reminding us to be inventive in our preparation of these vegetables. We boil the greens in water to cover, until they are tender but still bright, using the water for soups, so that no minerals will be lost.

The middle zone of man, where breathing and blood circulation are situated, corresponds to the leafy part in plants. This zone plays a decisive role in health and illness. Scientist Rudolf Hauschka explained: "The first reaction a person has on coming into the presence of a green sea of foliage after sole contact with the rocky earth element is to take a deep breath. The breathing organism is stimulated when we enter a green forest and sense the breathing going on there in the foliage. A leafy diet has the same result. Trees are the earth's lungs, and rustling leaves their breathing."[1]

When I stand in line at the supermarket with a big bunch of these vibrant, dark leaves, curious shoppers frequently ask how to cook them. Some have never seen them, while others offer stories and recipes from their grandmother who knew their value. Autumnal energy is held in the vegetables that thrive in the cool weather of this season. See how you feel with the daily use of vegetables.

While fall activites keep us outwardly busy, we can also experience the inside of autumn. Autumn's plaintive song sings of the turning inward of the earth. By listening for this song, we too, like the earth, prepare for the darkness of winter.

WINTER

OUR LIFE ENERGY REQUIRES A REST EVERY YEAR. We respond to the energy of winter by storing and replenishing our own energy during this darker time of the year. The garden is dormant, its vegetation in a state of maximum rest, and a "Do not disturb" sign hangs on the garden fence. The Chinese ancients suggest that, in winter, the will should also remain dormant, as if hiding or pretending, "not unlike someone with all his desires already fulfilled."[1]

Holding this thought over many winters, I have noticed that when I follow the natural desire to go inward in winter, I feel prepared and eager to meet spring, with plenty of energy both physically and creatively. On the other hand, I have also experienced winters when I did not take sufficient time to be quiet. Spring would come knocking on my door before I was ready, and I would long to pull the bedcovers over my head for another month's rest. Fatigue, flus, and colds, as well as late winter depression, can be repercussions of not respecting the powerful storehouse period of winter.

The parties and social events around December and January frequently result in low energy during the following month. One must be alert to balance celebrations with the need for reflective time. Through observation, we can learn how to move with the deep, slower rhythm of winter.

Midwinter festivals of light and the sun have been celebrated for thousands of years in the Americas, parts of Asia and ancient Egypt. These festivals bring light into our homes and our souls. Winter depression can occur if these inner fires are not lit. Knowing the art of how to create festivals that nourish us is particularly important during this season.

One winter, we were especially caught up in a flurry of school functions and parties with friends and relatives, in addition to preparations for the holidays. The children seemed tired, and one day, I became concerned when I noticed that our normally vivacious, laughing six-year-old looked deeply sad. After cancelling a visit with friends, we created our own ceremony of lights that evening. Both Maya and Zoe showed signs of relief as well as anticipation. We gathered all the candles in the house, placing them in the girls' bedroom. Their light cast a shimmering radiance on the walls, and I watched a softening occur in my daughters' faces. We sang songs about light, spirit, and the mysterious awe of this season. They asked for a story. There was such calm in the room that they both fell asleep just as I finished.

The next morning I was stunned. The girls were bright and happy, looking forward to Christmas with great delight. It was clear to me that such simple ceremonies can be very powerful in our lives.

Ceremonies of light show us a way to cultivate inner spiritual light at the darkest time of year. These ceremonies help to counter both the external darkness of the season and the internal darkness within one's own being.

The Water phase is most apparent in winter. We can experience the quality of Water both outwardly, in cold and wet weather, and inwardly, in the fluids in our body. The organs associated with the Water phase are the kidneys and bladder, and the adrenals, located just above the kidneys. In the Middle Ages, the kidneys were known as the seat of feelings and affections. The kidneys and the bladder are both vulnerable to cold and can be injured by excess cold or dampness.

Winter is an energy-building time for these organs if they are properly nourished. According to Oriental medicine, the kidneys store the life force, just as bulbs buried in the soil store energy during the winter. Known as "the Gates of Life," the kidneys provide energy for the entire system, and therefore are greatly respected. The kidneys store several types of energy, one of which is described as "ancestral energy." Present at birth, it supplies us for a full life-time unless we abuse it; then it is indeed hard to replenish.

We support ourselves through the cold and darkness by eating warming, strengthening foods. Hearty stews, thick with root vegetables like carrots, parsnips, and turnips, as well as the round vegetables, such as onions, squashes, and pumpkins, nourish our kidneys and, indeed, our whole systems. Good winter foods also include thick bean soups, hardy green winter vegetables, grain cereals for breakfast, lunches of substantial sandwiches using whole-grain breads, and miso soup. Sea vegetables are helpful if we feel depleted and low in minerals.

Cold winters can be a trying time for some vegetarians. Baking and sautéing plus the use of gentle spices, such as ginger root, generates warmth and energy to our bodies. This is a time to decrease consumption of cold or cooling foods, such as raw fruits or cold drinks. Some people enjoy the comforting qualities of buckwheat in winter, either as a whole grain or in noodles or pancakes.

In winter, I feel warmer when I occasionally include food such as fish stews or chicken soup. I recognize, after many years of mainly vegetarian eating, that the animal kingdom has medicinal value and is useful when we find ourselves unable to transform vegetarian food into sufficient fuel.

Let your intuition guide you in choosing the appropriate amount of salad or lightly sautéed or steamed vegetables. These foods play an important part in balancing weightier winter fare. Cooked seasonal fruits can be made into cobblers, crisps, pies, and puddings and offer us natural sweetness this time of year.

The flavor connected to winter and the Water phase is salty, so winter provides an opportunity to learn about our body's need for this vital mineral. The proper amount of salt is different for everyone and depends upon our physical condition, as well as our past intake of salt and meat.

Sufficient salt intake plays a particularly important role in maintaining strength in people who have been vegetarian for many years. Yet it should be

116

used cautiously by people with heart disease and a history of a high-fat, high-sodium eating, or for those who have consumed too much salt on a vegetarian diet.

Good quality sea salt contains more than eighty trace minerals in addition to sodium chloride. Most commercial table salt is a demineralized and bleached substance, containing mainly sodium chloride and additives. The body absorbs salt more easily when we cook with it, rather than sprinkling it on our food at the table. When cooked, it mixes with the substance of the food, and does not seem to stimulate the body in the same way.

Salt has a strong contracting energy that may create equally strong cravings toward expansion. If we eat too much or regularly add it uncooked to our food, we may naturally try to balance it with foods or liquids that have an expanding, relaxing, and if used in excess, weakening effect, such as fruit juices, beer, fruits, sugar, and ice cream. The pub owners in England understand this relationship and always sell salty snacks with alcoholic drinks; stimulating thirst results in more sales. This seesaw effect excites the taste buds but, over time, is taxing on the body.

A basic guideline for determining how much salt we need is to observe if we are thirsty after we eat. If we need more than a cup of tea or water after a meal, then it's likely that we are using too much. I went through just such a period and, while it gave me energy, prolonged overuse had a tightening effect that created a rigidity of thinking and a lack of fluidity in my body and emotions. Careful observation about our use of this crystal teaches us about its power.

In the darkness we prepare for the light of the coming spring. During this process, the self takes a back seat in our lives as we yield to something greater. This movement from winter to spring is a natural rhythm, like all seasons.

PART VI

PASSING THE FIRE

NOURISHING THE CHILD

The White Buffalo Woman showed the people how to use the pipe. She filled it with chan-shasha, red willow-bark tobacco. She walked around the lodge four times after the manner of Anpetu-Wi, the great sun. This represented the circle without end, the sacred hoop, the road of life. The woman placed a dry buffalo chip on the fire and lit the pipe with it. This was peta-owihankeshni, the fire without end, the flame to be passed on from generation to generation. She told them that the smoke rising from the bowl was Tunkashila's breath, the living breath of the great Grandfather Mystery.[1]

LAME DEER

 IN ANCIENT TIMES, the sacred flame was passed from one household to another, from mother to daughter. Today we pass the fire to our own children, even though we ourselves may only now be awakening to the importance of the sacred fire in our lives.

The daily rhythms of life and simply the way we are can be the glowing coals we pass to our children, the spark that brings light to those parts of ourselves that long to know the sacred. This chapter is about everyday life with children. It is also about us.

When our daughter, Zoe, was four years old, she told me a dream in which she entered a dark cave and found a fearsome dragon. She fought with the dragon, and hamburgers poured from his mouth, hitting her and her companions. Instead of shooting fire from his nostrils, he sprayed cans of Coca-Cola at everyone.

Her dream alerted me to my own dragons. I had unconsciously taught our

121

daughter to put foods into categories of good and evil. The evil foods were to be feared because they could cause illness. I realized that I needed to work on the way I communicated with our four-year-old. I knew that I wanted to teach our children about nutrition, but Zoe's dream warned me against using an approach that arose from my own mental constructs.

Most of what we eat today is vastly different from the foods available a hundred years ago. Our food is grown with pesticides that leave residues, packaged with preservatives, and is "refined" to be more marketable. Vitamins and minerals are stripped during processing and then added back in synthetic forms. Food is promoted to us through the media, stimulating our senses but bypassing our common sense. How could I show our children a more natural and instinctive approach to eating without filling them with fear?

After moving to the country, we started a vegetable garden and grew much of our own food. I gradually recognized that the most important lessons for children about food and nourishment come from their parents' own approach to food—how it is spoken of, prepared, handled, and eaten. A reverence for food and a sense of celebration at mealtimes has a healthy influence on the future eating habits of our children.

One year we grew a small plot of wheat. Maya and Zoe harvested and threshed it themselves. Then, with their father Stephen, they baked a couple of loaves of bread with the freshly ground flour. We had been talking about how the wheat needed the elements of earth, water, fire, and air (or metal, in the Chinese tradition) in order to grow. Stephen suggested to the girls that they find the elements and put them on their nature table. They arranged a glass of water, a crystal, a coin, a candle, and a few stalks of Stone Age wheat, an ancient variety that we grew for its beauty.

A few weeks later I watched six-year-old Zoe play with a friend. With great excitement, they prepared a banquet for the wedding of two dolls. An upturned shoe box became a table shimmering with beauty—flowers, ferns, acorns, and little bowls filled with bits of broken cookies arranged as offerings to the new bride and groom from all the animals. Sacred cookies? I would not have thought of that.

Early childhood educators such as Joseph Chilton Pearce, Jean Piaget, and Rudolf Steiner have stressed the need for parents to learn how to communicate with their young children. Premature use of intellectual or conceptual discussions with a young child can damage the child's future sense of well-being. Children develop according to natural cycles, and we can better assist them when we understand how these cycles unfold.

After nine months of gestation in the mother's rhythmic womb, the infant enters into a comparatively rhythmless daily chaos. The first thing the baby does is draw breath and rhythm is restored—in and out, in and out.

We can reinforce the child's inner rhythms during this time by offering an outer rhythm, which, during the first seven years of life, can give the child's soul and spirit a sense of security. We can establish rituals in a uniform sequence, little by little. The daily rhythm might involve waking up in the morning, making the bed, a blessing at meals, a story or song or candle at night, a prayer before going to sleep, and finally, a goodnight kiss. There may be a different rhythm for weekends. Seasons, festivals, and the annual birthday are longer, slower rhythms that also help orient the child.

Until about age seven, the child does not distinguish between inner and outer worlds. The atmosphere of a home, including the thoughts of the adults who live there, are absorbed by the child. This is especially true for the first three or four years of life. The child enjoys everything around him as if it were his own inner nature. I remember watching Zoe when she was four years old. Soon after she woke one morning, we went outside to feel the sun. "I love the smell of morning," she said, and her whole body quivered with the delight of the cool air, the fragrance of the jasmine flowers, the sounds of the birds. She *was* the morning.

Young children appreciate nature and enjoy stories that include images of all that they see around them. The stories can feature animals, their habitats, and the foods they eat in different seasons. Through nature a parent teaches a sense of wonder, the power of observation, and a feeling for the rhythms of nature.

Rudolf Steiner described this process: "The child comes to know of the plant world as belonging to the earth. He no longer merely stands on the dead ground of the earth, but he stands on the living ground, for he feels the earth as something alive. He gradually comes to think of himself standing on the ground as though he were standing on some great living creature, like a whale. This is right feeling. This alone can lead him to a really human feeling about the whole world."[2]

Everything we share with children can be approached in this manner.

Teaching through nature is most rewarding when we follow the child's lead. Rather than talking about food and its relationship to nature, we need only create a space for the magic to work. I took a walk with Maya one spring evening. It was dark, but there was a full moon to light our way. As we wove in and out of the shadows of towering redwoods, she noticed that she could feel the gentle moonlight on her face when we left the shadows. A few weeks later, when there was a quarter moon, she said that she could no longer feel the moonlight on her face. This made a deep impression on her and she was joyful in her realization that she could feel the full moon.

"One must feel nature," wrote Sufi mystic Hazrat Inayat Khan. "There is so much to be learned from plant life, from birds, from animals, and insects, that once a child begins to take an interest in that subject, everything becomes a symbolical expression of the inner truth."[3]

STORY RHYTHMS

You must know that there is nothing higher and stronger and more wholesome and good for life in the future than some good memory, especially a memory of childhood, of home. People talk to you a great deal about your education, but some good sacred memory, preserved from childhood, is perhaps the best education. If a man carries many such memories with him into life, he is safe to the end of his days, and if one has only one good memory left in one's heart, even that may be the means of saving us.[1]

DOSTOEVSKY
THE BROTHERS KARAMAZOV

 I DON'T EVEN REMEMBER the question I asked him. It's no longer important. But I did ask a specific question and naturally expected an answer. I had arranged for an interview with Efraim, the historian of the Cuna Indians who live on the San Blas Islands off the coast of Panama, but I got a whole lot more that evening.

Efraim was an oral historian and I was a journalist. I waited for him to answer my question, but he went on to tell story after story. Nearly three hours later, Efraim was still talking. I was exhausted and exasperated, wondering how to tell him politely that I wanted to go home to bed. I had long ago given up on the interview. And then, with clarity and distinction, he suddenly answered my question. I realized that every story he told me had been a precise and essential piece of the entire three-hour jigsaw puzzle. He smiled, and relaxed after a job well done. I felt very small.

To see the nature of one's mind can come as something of a shock. While

Efraim danced with the nuances of oral tradition, I was fixed on the goal and couldn't join in the dance. The color and texture of his answer was like mahogany, full, rich, mysterious; I had wanted an answer like thin, pale plywood.

I hungered for stories after I met Efraim. Stories feed us; they are born from myths and reflect the depths of our own unconscious. Stories help us to understand ourselves. One day I heard a storyteller on a public radio station. Her name was Sandra MacLees and I called the station to find out where I could write to her. To my delight, she had just moved to my area. Wasting no time, I called Sandra, told her I wanted to learn how to tell a story, and asked if she would show me. She agreed and so began our weekly meeting with a small group of friends. It was of little consequence whether the stories came from ourselves or from books. Once a story was chosen, it began to work on the teller, stirring and rousing those hidden places within each of us that wanted to wake up. After six weeks, we learned to trust that unfamiliar part of ourselves that holds our stories.

We each have a storyteller inside of us. It rises from a source of creativity that may take awhile to discover but, rest assured, it is there. Though at first your story may sound primitive to you, with practice, you will open up the place within you that resonates with a child's soul. No matter how simple the story, you will have access to this place where a child, in his deepest being, is quite at home.

Storytelling can be a little daunting. It's not structured like reading, and we have to, literally, face our audience. I stumbled along when I started and considered my initial efforts quite feeble. The symbolic world of stories was so nourishing to my children, however, that they supported and guided me with their comments and responses during my early attempts to learn the art.

Don't feel you have to put a moral in every story. It's far more nourishing to just tell the story as it comes. Trust that your internal storyteller will guide you to say things that are appropriate for the moment. Storytelling brings you into a new realm where you communicate symbolically, through fantasy and images. It provides a breathing space, a context within which children can work things out for themselves.

An experienced teacher of young children, Dr. Caroline Von Heydebrand, gave this advice to storytellers fifty years ago: Little stories should be as simple as possible, but dramatic and full of life. The moral should speak only from the events portrayed and not be added as an abstract maxim at the end. The children should not feel the story to be directed at themselves by any emphasis in the telling of it; this would only upset and depress them. It should be left to them to find any application to their own shortcomings. That they do this is often given away by their innocent exclamations. For example, after a dramatic description of an inattentive child, a child might say "I am not like that! I would never say such a thing!" showing that the story has gone home.[2]

Once you begin, the joy of storytelling awakens within you. You will surprise yourself by what comes out. When is a good time to tell a story? Whenever a situation calls for it. The following story was born out of my own impatience and irritation. We had to get to an appointment, and the children were dawdling; Maya began to cry and Zoe was angry at my pushing. This was a pattern we seemed to fall into time after time.

The Fairy Diamond

Once upon a time there was a turtle, Mrs. Turtle was her name, and she made her home in a very large tree stump. Around the stump was a garden filled with flowers and vegetables, and a large lavender bush stood at her door. Inside were all sorts of herbs and roots and leaves, dried and fresh, fragrant and plain. She loved to examine all of her plants daily; she watered them, smelled them, and nibbled on the tasty ones.

One day Mrs. Turtle was invited to have tea and cakes with Mrs. Owl. Their friend, Mrs. Rabbit, was also invited. Mrs. Turtle started to get ready for this tea party very early in the morning, but, you know, Mrs. Turtle moved so slowly that by lunch time she had only begun to spruce herself up and shine her shell. She didn't have much to do to get ready for the party, but what she did do took her quite awhile. She was so careful and so slow.

Dinnertime arrived and Mrs. Turtle still wasn't ready. She was putting on her gloves and making sure that everything was just right. She was giving her shell the finishing touch with a soft cloth when she heard a rustling outside. She went across to the window and saw that it was Mrs. Rabbit, all ready to go to Mrs. Owl's party!

Mrs. Rabbit had fluffed up her tail with pink powder, combed and sleeked her fur, and curled her whiskers. She said to Mrs. Turtle, "It's time to go to the tea party! I'm on my way. Would you like to join me?"

"Oh no," said Mrs. Turtle, "I couldn't do that, as I'm not quite ready."

"Well then," replied Mrs. Rabbit, "I shall simply have to see you there!"

And off she scampered, arriving at Mrs. Owl's tree in no time at all. Mrs. Turtle, on the other hand, was still fixing her gloves and looking for her favorite hat made out of leaves. (She had made it, thinking she could eat it if she got hungry on an outing.) She looked out the window when she thought she heard Mrs. Owl's hooting. To her surprise, she saw the moon rising like an orange in the sky.

"Oh, I must be going now, I suppose," said Mrs. Turtle out loud. "It's time I went to the tea party." Finally, she was ready. She started out the door, but ever so slowly. She crawled on all fours, since that's what turtles do, and went crunching over twig, leaf, and grass at a slow but steady pace.

The moon was rising higher and higher, and Mrs. Turtle was only halfway there. She continued on, looking at leaves and bugs along the way. Suddenly she saw something directly in front of her, lying on the ground. It glowed and gleamed and sparkled with a million colors and lights. She got closer, and do you know what? Mrs. Turtle found a real diamond. She stopped and simply bathed in its light. "I think I will put that in my pocket and show it to Mrs. Owl, as she always knows about these sorts of things," thought Mrs. Turtle to herself.

By the time Mrs. Turtle arrived at Mrs. Owl's party, the moon had already slipped behind the trees, and it was nearly midnight. The house was silent and all the guests had gone. The teacups were put away, and the last crumbs of the tea cakes were carried off by Mrs. Mouse who said she would give them to her little ones.

Mrs. Owl was expecting Mrs. Turtle. She never slept much at night anyway. When she heard crunching sounds as Mrs Turtle moved up the path, Mrs. Owl came to her door. "Good evening, dear Turtle," said Mrs. Owl. "I think you missed the tea party. But do come in anyway, and let us have a cup of rosemary tea together."

Mrs. Turtle could barely wait until she got inside to tell Mrs. Owl all about the diamond she found. But first she remembered Mrs. Rabbit. "Did Rabbit get to the party?" asked Mrs. Turtle.

"Oh yes, and she ate many carrot buns and had a very nice time."

"Oh good," thought Mrs. Turtle to herself, thinking how quickly Mrs. Rabbit had dressed herself and ran over to Owl's tree.

"I am sorry I couldn't get here on time," she said to Mrs. Owl.

And then, Mrs. Turtle took out the gleaming diamond, and showed

Mrs. Owl who said "ooooh" and "aaaaah" and things like that, nodding her head very gravely. "Do you know this is a diamond and not just any diamond, but a fairy's diamond?" said Mrs. Owl. "You get three wishes that will last you for the rest of your life."

Mrs. Turtle was most surprised. She had found a diamond, and would never go hungry now! Do you know what she wished for? First she wished that all her fellow creatures would live happily in the forest. Second, she wished that she would always have enough leaves to eat, and that no fire would ever burn up her plants. And third, she wished that one day she could fly, as fast as a swallow. She wanted to know what it felt like to soar through the air. She knew she was a turtle, and because she was a turtle she was able to find a tiny diamond that had dropped out of a fairy's hand onto the forest floor. Any other animal would have missed it, for it had been hidden among the moss and leaves. But she still wanted to know what it felt like to fly.

And Mrs. Turtle and Mrs. Owl spent the rest of the night together. They had tea and talked until dawn. Tired out, they watched in silence as a beautiful sunrise turned from deep crimson to a pink blush. Mrs. Turtle went home that morning, and returned the diamond to the very spot were she had found it. This is what you do with fairy diamonds. She said her three wishes, and then left the diamond for someone else, who, someday, may be lucky enough to find it.

Symbols can help us to transform the energy of the psyche. When we are stuck in a particular way of thinking, a symbol, whether in a dream, a story, or a drawing, can literally break apart our rigidity. It frees us to take a more responsive approach to life.

Storytelling is not only for the listeners. It works on the teller as well.

By the end of my story, my impatience had melted into a deeper respect for my children. I softened my attitude to their timing and going out became easier for us all.

One rainy, cold winter day, the girls and I made a trip to the local grocery store. It was about half an hour before dinner. They watched a man giving ice cream on a stick to his children. The girls wanted one, too. I told them no, it was too close to dinner. They demanded to know why they couldn't have ice cream then and there, just like the other children. "Why?" did not go away.

Not only did I not want them to spoil their dinner, I didn't want them eating ice cream in this cold weather. Their question, I sensed, was deeper than a simple request to eat ice cream. It was a demand to know why we didn't eat like the kids in television commercials or like those other children in the store. Why were we different? A simple "no" wasn't going to do for an answer.

I said I would tell them a story in answer to their question. They were six and two at the time, and at the mention of a story they came to attention. I said we would wait until we got into the car. The girls' questioning stopped in anticipation.

I made an inner plea for inspiration. This was the birth of the Eduardo stories. I remembered a friend who worked as a forest ranger in Yosemite National Park. He had told us that the wild animals were adversely affected by the foods that campers sometimes fed them, and described to us how the coats of the bear and deer became rough and mangy instead of glossy and silky. A story was in the making, and out it came. It was the story of Eduardo the Squirrel, who lived in a forest with his family in a multi-storied nest.

The children were transfixed by this story. When I finished, I knew they were somehow satisfied. "Tell me an Eduardo story" became a frequent request, and over the next few years I told dozens of them.

I saw that what nourished the children was the repetition of these stories.

New stories were fine sometimes, but what they really wanted was the rhythm of hearing the same familiar characters in different settings. They even began to tell their own Eduardo stories as they grew older.

The storyteller needs to know which stories to repeat and which ones to let go. How will we know this? Be assured that our young audience will always let us know if we become attached to our own stories. "Not that again," they will moan. The balance between freshness and the comfort of repetition is ours to discover.

One day Eduardo wanted to go exploring, so he told his parents he was going out for the day. He climbed up a branch, leapt across to another branch, then jumped to the next tree. He climbed and jumped from tree to tree for quite awhile until he grew tired. Just then a shiny, black raven flew by, and asked if Eduardo wanted a ride to a beautiful meadow. Eduardo said "Yes," and climbed onto the bird's back.

They flew high above the trees. Eduardo felt as if he were skimming the clouds. Finally the raven saw the spot he was looking for, and together they landed in a green meadow full of wildflowers. They saw many, many deer. The deer were having a celebration. They had discovered some food left by campers and were having a wonderful time eating doughnuts, cookies, sandwich bread, and other goodies. The food was so sweet and tasty, and there was so much of it that they decided to stop eating berries and nuts.

By the next winter, however, they were cold. Many of the deer lost their thick coats of hair. The younger deer stood shivering and forlorn when the snow fell. No one knew what to do until one day the deer parents decided to ask Grandmother Deer how they could keep their children warm. Grandmother Deer was very old, and she had seen many generations of deer. She thought and thought about this, and here's what she said: "If you want your beautiful sleek coats back, you must eat what Mother Nature will provide next spring. Until then, you must walk close to your children, always keeping them warm."

When spring came the deer returned to eating their berries, fresh leaves, and nuts, and their coats grew thick and glossy. They still loved to eat the leftovers from human campers, and did so occasionally, but they didn't forget Grandmother Deer's words.

Eduardo returned home after that year, and told his family many stories about all that he saw. They were so happy to have him back that they held a party for him. There was fresh acorn stew, nut jello, and berry pie. Eduardo was pleased to be back home.

Once when Maya and I were reminiscing over stories I had told the girls, she said, "And I'll tell my little girl Eduardo stories when I am a mother. And she will say to her child, 'Your great-grandmother Anne used to tell these stories, and now I will tell them to you.' "

We laughed as we elaborated on the image of great-grandmother Anne, but in truth, I was uneasy. As we talked, for just a moment, I didn't exist except in the memory of future children. And then, abruptly, I was back in my car, driving Maya to her grandmother's house. In that split-second crack between now and the future, I saw the full power of ritual and the hearth. It can be deadening and imprisoning, or, used freely, it can transmit love through time.

You can start tonight, if you haven't already started telling stories. But remember that it's not so much the words in a story that children need but the communication that goes from heart to heart. This holds them securely in place.

Close the door, so it's just you and your child. Light a candle; feel the sweetness and mystery of night. This is a practice, a ritual of the hearth; it links you to the nighttime storytelling that has existed around the fire since ancient times. Before you start, close your eyes. Ask in your heart for a story to be told through you. One that is just right for your child, tonight. And then begin.

Of course, you don't need to have children of your own to begin story-telling. When a story wants to be told, it always finds the right listeners.

PART VII

FULL CIRCLE

HESTIA'S SONG

NOURISHMENT HAS INTELLIGENCE of its own; it goes where it's most needed. It touches us quite impersonally, but leaves its mark in a most personal way, showing us how to be present in time. Nourishment calls us into the ordinary, into daily life, by giving meaning to what we do. This was shown to me one very special day.

I step out of the house for a quick walk, slotted between seeing a client and carpool duties. I am no more than three minutes into a brisk pace when I pass by a creek in a ravine. It beckons to me. I stop, undecided for a moment whether to let myself enjoy this peaceful spot, or to walk on and get my exercise. The creek wins. I gingerly climb down a fallen redwood tree that bridges the water flowing ten feet below me. Much of the sunlight is blocked by tall bay trees, but I can just fit in a small patch of dappled light if I sit cross-legged at the base of the tree.

"The walk would be better for you," interrupts my mind. But the thought goes limp as I sit there, looking at the ferns, the wild ginger. I close my eyes, and listen instead of look.

My ears are hungry, wanting to feed on the sounds that I can now hear. Two noisy scrub jays, a squirrel scurrying to get somewhere, leaping around the branches and then becoming quiet. A mockingbird trills beautiful, long sequences of notes. I begin to exhale when it begins its song, and am surprised to find that the bird can sing longer than my exhalation. Do mockingbirds take imperceptibly quick in-breaths in between notes? I'm amused at the thought, but realize I have stopped listening.

I go deeper, and the sounds draw me in until I am no longer aware of sitting by the creek. I later realize I have to check my watch. I'm startled to find

137

that a half hour has gone by, and it's time to go. It's hard to leave. I feel as if I am being held. A sweet fullness lingers all afternoon and lasts for days. Something has happened.

For years I have disliked carpool duties, but I notice in the car that afternoon that driving carpool is fine. The hard edges that I always feel are not there; there's no subtle irritation, no wishing I was doing something else. I'm curious. It can't last. But it does, and I detect that whatever was keeping me from being present while driving carpool has now been healed. Two years have passed, and I still wonder about the magic of that afternoon.

I once had a dream about Hestia, goddess of the hearth. In the dream, I am learning the lines for a play about Hestia. I simply could not remember the lines. I am then shown a film about Hestia. She is a magnificent and beautiful goddess, sensuous and earthy. She sings, "All is the light, the light is all," but she is weeping, for people have forgotten her. A nun appears in the dream, shocked by Hestia's sensuality, and says sharply to me, "You had better not play Hestia like that!" But I know that I have seen the real Hestia. I realize that I don't need to learn the lines; just to sing her song is enough.

The dream startled me. I never expected Hestia to look so stunning. In my unconscious I had shreds of a devalued image of Hestia, perhaps just a little frumpy, a little less than powerful. This was a far cry from my image of the starving girl many years ago, but the dream revealed that I was still unable to allow aspects of my own nature to be nourished. The resplendence of Hestia in my dream burned away ancient remnants of shame about the feminine. This Hestia was gorgeous, rejoicing in the splendor of her body, divine, yet of the earth.

When an archetype plays strongly in our lives, it's important to understand that we don't identify with the archetype, but rather form a relationship with it. It is a living energy that can enrich our lives, not a stereotype that affixes us to a specific design. For me, the archetype that I discovered in my dream offered me a sense of freedom that allowed me to expand my understanding of the sacred nature of the feminine.

The archetypes of Hermes, Hestia, Pele, Gabija, and Brighde can guide us in the ways of the hearth; we learn how to honor the sacred without losing our humanity. The fire goddesses reveal to us what it means to live in two worlds, to know our divine nature but still cook breakfast on Monday morning.

We are human and we make mistakes; but, held by our love for the sacred, we are able to recognize our own failings and imperfections, and to see them as precious. They are part of the fire that burns and purifies us so that we can ultimately hear the song of our soul.

THE RACCOON STORY

I KNOW A WOMAN WHO COOKS DINNER every night for a raccoon. She puts her leftovers between two pieces of bread. The sandwich is placed in a plastic bag that the woman buries under a foot of dirt in her backyard. She leaves a couple of inches of the bag sticking out of the ground. Over this goes a pot to keep other animals from taking the food. Later in the evening, a raccoon comes to get his dinner. He's been coming for over two years now. The woman is a widow. Her husband died just a little over two years ago. She feeds the raccoon. He feeds her.

Love burns away distinctions between giver and receiver as nourishment becomes a circle. The food we make with our hands, all that we do, ultimately becomes an expression of this inner mystery. But where there's love, the world is no longer us and them. We become part of the circle, and that is both sublime and terrifying.

When we offer ourselves to the fire, to the hearth, there is a high price to pay; love asks that we give all of ourselves, even the parts that we would rather keep away from the fire. That's why we try to bargain with love, or hope it will be a part-time job. But, if we have tasted its sweetness, even just once, then we have already lost our bargaining position.

Rumi wrote, "The mystery of loving is God's sweetest secret."[1] Love is the ultimate nourishment, the One behind all the others. And yet, joyful as it is, the gift of being purely ourselves is not given for ourselves. We are given this mysterious nourishment so that we can weave it into our lives, in the daily routine, in the marketplace, so that it can be woven into the fabric of the world.

CHAPTER NOTES

Part I: Sacred Fire

THE GIFT OF THE BUDDHIST COOK

1. Coleman Barks and John Moyne, *Open Secret, Versions of Rumi,* p. 19.

FIRE IN THE HEARTH

1. Mechtild of Magdeburg, quoted by Carol Lee Flinders, *Enduring Grace,* p. 58.
2. Alexander Carmichael, *Carmina Gadelica,* p. 236-237.

FIRE GODDESSES

1. Marion Woodman, *Conscious Femininity,* p. 19.
2. Marija Gimbutas, personal communication, 1989.
3. Sinead Sula Grian, *Brighde, Goddess of Fire,* p. 1.
4. Ibid., p. 7.
5. Ibid., p. 19.
6. Ibid., p. 4.
7. Ibid., p. 5.
8. Cicero, quoted by Dumezil, in Barbara Walker, *The Woman's Encyclopedia of Myths and Secrets,* p. 400.
9. Dr. Peter Kingsley, personal communication, April 17, 1994, and Peter Kingsley Ph.D., *Ancient Philosophy, Mystery and Magic,* chapters 13-14.
10. Stobaeus, describing Philolaus, quoted by Carl A. Huffman, *Philolaus of Croton: Pythagorean and Presocratic,* p. 226-227.
11. Kingsley, personal communication.
12. Karl Kerenyi, *Hermes, Guide of Souls,* p. 84.
13. Jean Shinoda Bolen, *Goddesses in Everywoman,* p. 115

TENDING THE HEARTH

1. W. R. Lethaby, quoted by Walker, *The Woman's Encyclopedia of Myths and Secrets,* p. 400.

Part II: Rhythms and Rituals of the Hearth

THE MOUTH OF A MONK IS LIKE AN OVEN
1. Dogen Zenji, quoted in *Macrobiotics Today,* p. 20.
2. Soei Yoneda, *Good Food from a Japanese Temple,* p. 35.
3. Dogen Zenji and Kosho Uchiyama Roshi, *Refining Your Life,* p. 13.

RITUAL IN THE KITCHEN
1. Joseph Campbell, *The Power of Myth,* p. 84-85.
2. Informal talk in Sebastopol, CA, November, 1990 with Shaykh Tosun Bayrak of the Helveti Jerrahi Order of America, Spring Valley, NY.

SETTING IT STRAIGHT
1. W.A. Mathieu, *The Listening Book,* p. 123.

GREETING DRAGONS RESPECTFULLY
1. Rocky Olguin, "Listening to Native American Women."

THE CUTTING EDGE
1. Gary Snyder, *Practice of the Wild,* p. 18.

COMING HOME
1. C.T. Onions, ed., *The Shorter Oxford English Dictionary.*

Part III: Sweeping the Hearth

ANCESTORS OF THE HEARTH
1. Thich Nhat Hanh, *Touching Peace,* p. 31.

COAXING HABITS
1. Mark Twain, *Pudd'nhead Wilson,* p. 51.

THE FOOD OF DREAMS

1. Quoted by Llewellyn Vaughan-Lee, *The Lover and the Serpent,* p. 23.

BODY RHYTHMS

1. Hazrat Inayat Khan, *Healing and the Mind World,* p. 74.

THE BROKEN HEARTH

1. M.F.K. Fisher, *The Gastronomical Me,* quoted by Carol Lee Flinders, *Enduring Grace,* p. xi.

Part IV: Table Rhythms

THE MYSTERY OF EATING

1. Joseph Campbell, quoting from *The Upanishads* in *The Power of Myth,* p. 173.
2. Rudolf Steiner, "The Kingdoms of Nature and of Spiritual Beings," *The Universe, Earth and Man,* p. 45.
3. Larry Dossey, *Space, Time & Medicine,* p. 215.
4. Eknath Easwaran, *The Bhagavad Gita,* p. 135.

CELEBRATION AND RITUAL

1. Quoted by Michel Abehsera, "The Sabbath Meal," p. 14.
2. Sara Wenger Shenk, *Why Not Celebrate!,* p. 20.

AROUND THE POI BOWL

1. Dainin Katagiri, *Returning to Silence,* p. 1.

CHEWING PRACTICE

1. Swami Muktananda, from *Reflections of the Self,* quoted by Lino Stanchich, *Power Eating Program,* p. 31.
2. Edmond Szekely, *The Essene Gospel of Peace,* p. 55.
3. Noburo Muramoto, *Natural Immunity,* p. 141.
4. Michel Abehsera, p. 14-15.

BLESSINGS

1. Beverly Hungry Wolf, *The Ways of My Grandmothers,* p. 189.
2. Dogen, quoted by Edward Espe Brown, "The Heart of Tassajara Cooking," in *EastWest,* p. 86.
3. Quoted from *The Upanishads,* by Linda Banchek, *Cooking for Life: Ayurvedic Recipes for Good Food and Good Health.*
4. John Bierhorst, ed., *The Sacred Path,* p. 119.
5. Edward Espe Brown, personal communication, September, 1989.

Part V: Earth Rhythms

THE FIVE PHASES

1. Marcus Aurelius, trans. by Maxwell Staniforth of *Marcus Aurelius Meditations.*
2. Dianne Connelly, *Traditional Acupuncture; The Law of the Five Elements,* p. 13.
3. Quoted by Ilza Veith, trans. of *The Yellow Emperor's Classic of Internal Medicine,* p. 136.

SPRING

1. Hugh Baker, *Ancestral Images,* p. 66.
2. Gerhard Schmidt, *The Essentials of Nutrition,* p. 252.

SUMMER

1. Christina Hole, *A Dictionary of British Folk Customs,* p. 207.
2. Dan Kenner, *Botanical Medicine: A European Perspective,* Part I.

AUTUMN

1. Rudolf Hauschka, *Nutrition,* p. 80.

WINTER

1. Dr. Henry Lu, *Chinese Diet for Your Health,* p. 17.

Part VI: Passing the Fire

NOURISHING THE CHILD

1. Richard Erdoes and Alfonso Ortiz, *American Indian Myths and Legends,* p. 49.
2. Rudolf Steiner, *The Kingdom of Childhood,* p. 65.
3. Hazrat Inayat Khan, *The Art of Personality,* p. 12.

STORY RHYTHMS

1. Fyodor Dostoevsky, *The Brother's Karamazov,* (The Great Books of the Western World, #52), p. 411.
2. Caroline Von Heydebrand, *Childhood, A Study of the Growing Soul,* p. 70.

Part VII: Full Circle

THE RACCOON STORY

1. Coleman Barks, *Feeling the Shoulder of the Lion,* p. 61.

Bibliography

Abehsera, Michel. "The Sabbath Meal" *Macromuse*. Bethesda, MD: Winter 1987.

Aurelius, Marcus. *Marcus Aurelius Meditations*. Translated by Maxwell Staniforth. London: Penguin Classics, 1964.

Baker, Hugh. *Ancestral Images*. Hong Kong: South China Morning Post, 1979.

Banchek, Linda. *Cooking for Life: Ayurvedic Recipes for Good Food and Good Health*. New York: Harmony Books, 1993.

Barks, Coleman. *Feeling the Shoulder of the Lion*. Putney, VT: Threshold Books, 1991.

—. and John Moyne, *Open Secret, Versions of Rumi*. Putney, VT: Threshold Books, 1984.

Beilenson, Nick, ed. *Table Graces*. Cambridge, UK: Lutterworth Press, 1986.

Bierhorst, John, *The Sacred Path*. New York: Quill, 1984.

Bolen, Jean Shinoda. *Goddesses in Everywoman*. New York: Harper & Row, 1984.

Britz-Crecelius, Heidi. *Children at Play: Preparation for Life*. Edinburgh: Floris Books, 1979.

Campbell, Joseph. *The Inner Reaches of Outer Space*. New York: Harper & Row, 1986.

—. *The Power of Myth*. New York: Doubleday, 1988.

Carmichael, Alexander. *Carmina Gadelica*. Edinburgh: T & A Constable, 1900.

Colbin, Annemarie. *Food and Healing*. New York: Ballantine Books, 1986.

Connelly, Dianne. *Traditional Acupuncture: The Law of the Five Elements*. Columbia, Maryland: The Centre for Traditional Acupuncture Inc.

Cook, Katsi. "Prenatal Nutrition: Some Old Indian Ways." *Daybreak,* Winter 1989.

Davy, Gudrun, and Bons Voors. *Lifeways*. Stroud, UK: Hawthorn. Press, 1983.

De Langre, Jacques. "The Value of Real Sea Salt," Magalia, CA: The Grain and Salt Society, 1993.

Dogen, Zenji, "Tenzo Kyokun: Instructions for the Zen Cook," *Macrobiotics Today*. Oroville, CA: George Ohsawa Macrobiotic Foundation, September 1989.

—. and Kosho Uchiyama Roshi. *Refining Your Life*. New York and Tokyo: John Weatherhill, Inc., 1983.

Dossey, Larry. *Space, Time & Medicine.* Boulder, CO: Shambala, 1982.

Dostoevsky, Fyodor. *The Brothers Karamazov* (The Great Books of the Western World, #52). Chicago: William Benton, 1952.

EastWest. "The Heart of Tassajara Cooking, an Interview with Edward Espe Brown." Boston: East West Partners, April 1986.

Easwaran, Eknath, translation of *The Bhagavad Gita.* Petaluma, CA: Nilgiri Press, 1985.

Erdoes, Richard, and Alfonso Ortiz, *American Indian Myths and Legends.* New York: Pantheon Books, 1984.

Flinders, Carol Lee. *Enduring Grace.* New York: HarperCollins, 1993.

Gimbutas, Marija. *The Goddesses and Gods of Old Europe.* Berkeley and Los Angeles: University of California Press, 1974, reprint London: Thames and Hudson, 1982.

—. "The Temples of Old Europe," *Archeology,* November/December, 1980.

Glockler, Michaela, and Wolfgang Goebel. *A Guide to Child Health.* Edinburgh: Floris Books, 1990.

Grian, Sinead Sula. *Brighde, Goddess of Fire.* Glastonbury, UK: Brighde's Fire, 1985.

Hauschka, Rudolf. *Nutrition.* London: Rudolf Steiner Press, 1951.

Hole, Christina. *A Dictionary of British Folk Customs.* London: Granada Publishing, 1976.

Huffman, Carl A. *Philolaus of Croton: Pythagorean and Presocratic.* Cambridge, UK: Cambridge University Press, 1993.

Hungry Wolf, Beverly. *The Ways of My Grandmothers.* New York: Quill 1982.

Jacobs, Heinrich. *Six Thousand Years of Bread.* New York: Doubleday, 1944.

Katagiri, Dainin. *Returning to Silence.* Boston: Shambhala Publications, 1988.

Kenner, Dan. *Botanical Medicine: A European Perspective.* Brookline: Paradigm Publications, (in press).

Kerenyi, Karl. *Hermes, Guide of Souls.* Dallas: Spring Publications, 1986.

Khan, Hazrat Inayat. *The Sufi Message of Hazrat Inayat Khan: Healing and the Mind World.* Netherlands: Servire BV, 1982.

—. *The Art of Personality.* Netherlands: Servire BV, 1982.

Kingsley, Peter. *Ancient Philosophy, Mystery and Magic*. Oxford, UK: Oxford University Press, (in press).

Konig, Karl. *The First Three Years of the Child*. Edinburgh: Floris Books, 1957.

Lu, Henry. *Chinese Diet for Your Health*. Vancouver, BC: The Academy of Oriental Heritage, 1980.

Mathieu, W.A. *The Listening Book*. Boston: Shambhala Publications, 1991.

Mohaghan, Patricia. *The Book of Goddesses & Heroines*. St. Paul, MN: Llewellyn Publications, 1990.

Muramoto, Noboru. *Natural Immunity*. Oroville, CA: George Ohsawa Macrobiotic Foundation, 1988.

Onions, C.T., ed. *The Shorter Oxford English Dictionary*. London: Oxford University Press, 1965.

Schmidt, Gerhard. *The Essentials of Nutrition*. Wyoming, Rhode Island: Bio-Dynamic Literature, 1979.

Shenk, Sara Wenger. *Why Not Celebrate!* Intercourse, PA: Good Books, 1987.

Snyder, Gary, *The Practice of the Wild*. Berkeley, CA: North Point Press, 1990.

Stanchich, Lino, *Power Eating Program*. Miami, FL: Healthy Products, Inc., 1989.

Steiner, Rudolf. *The Kingdom of Childhood*. London: Rudolf Steiner Press, 1982.

—. "The Kingdoms of Nature and of Spiritual Beings," *The Universe, Earth and Man*. London: Rudolf Steiner Press, 1982.

Szekely, Edmond Bordeaux. *The Essene Gospel of Peace*. Cartago, Costa Rica: International Biogenic Society, 1978.

Thich Nhat Hahn. *Touching Peace*. Berkeley, CA: Parallax Press, 1992.

Thomas, Heather. *Journey Through Time in Verse and Rhyme*. London: Rudolf Steiner Press, 1987.

Twain, Mark. *Pudd'nhead Wilson*. New York: New American Library, 1964.

Vaughan-Lee, Llewellyn. *The Lover and the Serpent*. Shaftesbury, UK: Element Books, 1990.

Veith, Ilza. *The Yellow Emperor's Classic of Internal Medicine*. (1949); reprinted by University of California Press, Berkeley and Los Angeles: 1966, 1972.

Von Heydebrand, Caroline. *Childhood, A Study of the Growing Soul*. London: Rudolf Steiner Press, 1970.

Walker, Barbara. *The Woman's Encyclopedia of Myths and Secrets.* San Francisco: Harper and Row, 1983.

—. *The Woman's Dictionary of Symbols & Sacred Objects.* San Francisco: Harper & Row, 1988.

Woodman, Marion. *Conscious Femininity.* Toronto: Inner City Books, 1993.

Wyatt, Isabel. *Seven-Year-Old Wonder-Book.* Sausalito, CA: Dawne-leigh Publications, 1975.

Yoneda, Soei. *Good Food from a Japanese Temple.* Tokyo: Kodansha International, 1982.